It's another Quality Book from CGP

*Want to hear the **bad news**? There's an awful lot of heavy-going stuff they expect you to learn for GCSE Religious Studies.*

*Want to hear the **good news**? Good old CGP have got it all covered! We've produced this brilliant book for the main options, with all the concepts beautifully explained in clear, simple English so you can understand it — and remember it.*

And then, in the spirit of going the extra mile, we've put in a smattering of not-so-serious bits to try and make the whole experience at least partly entertaining for you.

We've done all we can — the rest is up to you.

What CGP is all about

Our sole aim here at CGP is to produce the highest quality books — carefully written, immaculately presented and dangerously close to being funny.

Then we work our socks off to get them out to you — at the cheapest possible prices.

Key to Symbols and Bible / Qur'an References:

1. The clouds in section 1 tell you whether the page covers:

   (Christianity) the Christian view... (Judaism) ...the Jewish view... (Islam) ...the Muslim view...

   (General) ... or general views that <u>everyone</u> doing a perspectives option needs to learn.

2. In section 2 there's also a spiky blob to tell you you've reached the stuff about Mark's Gospel. You might not need that stuff, even if you do need the rest of the section. (GOSPEL)

3. References from the Bible always go in the order: *Book Chapter:Verse(s)*. So whenever you see something like: Mark 3:5-6, it means it's from the book of Mark, Chapter 3, verses 5-6. Similarly, references from the Qur'an are shown with the *Surah* (*Chapter*) followed by the *Ayat* (*Verse*).

Contents

Section One — Perspectives

Believing in God

Spirituality 1
The Nature of Truth 2
Believing in God 3
Religious Experiences 4
The Nature of God 5
Christian and Jewish Teaching on God 6
Muslim Teaching on God 7
Evil and Suffering 8
Judaism and Islam — Evil and Suffering 9
The Origin of the World 10

Life and Death

Life After Death 11
Jewish Beliefs about Life After Death 12
Muslim Beliefs about Life After Death 13
Life & Death and the Christian View 14
Life & Death in Judaism 16
Life & Death in Islam 17
Fertility Treatment 18
Revision Summary 19

Marriage and the Family

Marriage in Christianity 20
The Christian Church and Divorce 21
Marriage in Judaism 22
Marriage in Islam 23
Religious Attitudes to Sex 24
Children and the Church 25

Social Harmony

Prejudice and Equality 26
Race and Religion 27
Injustice and Protest 28
Jewish Attitudes towards Equality 29
Muslim Attitudes towards Equality 30
Christianity and Other Religions 31
Judaism, Islam and Other Religions 32
Revision Summary 33

Caring for Others

Christianity and Poverty 34
Judaism, Islam and Poverty 35
Religion and the Environment 36
Religion and Animals 37

Crime, War, Drugs, Media

Religion and Crime 38
Christianity and War 39
Judaism, Islam and War 40
Religion and Drugs 41
Religion and the Media 42
Revision Summary 44

Section Two — Christianity

Core Beliefs

- Basic Christian Beliefs ... 45
- The Bible ... 46
- Christian Values ... 47
- Love and Forgiveness ... 48
- The Sermon on the Mount ... 49
- Spreading the Gospel ... 50
- Living the Christian Life ... 51

The Church

- The Church ... 52
- Traditions and Denominations ... 53
- Members of the Church ... 55
- A Christian Church ... 56
- Religious Symbolism ... 58
- Revision Summary ... 59

Worship

- Sunday Worship ... 60
- Christian Festivals ... 61
- Private Prayer and the Sacraments ... 62
- Baptism ... 63
- Funerals, Burial and Cremation ... 64

Mark's Gospel

- Jesus and Mark's Gospel ... 65
- The Kingdom of God ... 66
- Jesus and Miracles ... 67
- Miracles, Faith and Conflict ... 68
- Discipleship ... 69
- Jesus' Trial and Death ... 70
- Revision Summary ... 71

Section Three — Judaism

- The Beginnings of Judaism ... 72
- Basic Jewish Beliefs ... 73
- Sources of Guidance ... 74
- The Holocaust ... 75
- Different Jewish Traditions ... 76
- Judaism and Day-to-Day Life ... 77
- The Synagogue ... 78
- Signs and Symbols ... 79
- Judaism and Children ... 80
- Jewish Beliefs about Death ... 81
- Jewish Prayer and the Sabbath ... 82
- Pilgrimage, Food and Fasting ... 83
- Jewish Festivals ... 84
- Revision Summary ... 85

Section Four — Islam

- Basic Islamic Beliefs ... 86
- Prophets and Angels ... 87
- The Qur'an ... 88
- The Prophet Muhammad ... 89
- Different Islamic Traditions ... 90
- Sufism ... 91
- Islam and the Shari'ah ... 92
- Islamic Living and Jihad ... 93
- The Mosque ... 94
- Worship and Prayer ... 95
- Birth and Death Ceremonies ... 97
- Revision Summary ... 98

Index ... 99

Published by: Coordination Group Publications Ltd

Contributors:
Stewart Bates-Treloar
Jill Hudson
Simon Little
John Nichols
Andy Park
Duncan Raynor
Glenn Rogers
Paul D. Smith
Nigel Thomas
Claire Thompson

ISBN 1-84146-190-3
Groovy Website: www.cgpbooks.co.uk

Printed by Elanders Hindson, Newcastle upon Tyne.
Clipart sources: CorelDRAW and VECTOR.
With thanks to Enid Thompson for some of the church photos.

Spirituality

General

Here we go then, with a right tricky page. What a way to start.

Spirituality isn't Necessarily to do with Religion

There are a couple of ways of defining spirituality:

a) *Concern with anything relating primarily to the spirit (or soul)*: this isn't necessarily to do with religion. Someone whose mind or emotions work on a 'higher plane' may be described as a spiritual person.

b) *An expression of faith*: anything relating to the way in which a religious person demonstrates his or her spiritual side — something which is built up through religious practice.

Spirituality is Hard to Put your Finger on

1) An important part of spirituality for many people (whether it's religious or not) is the search for the meaning of life. This may involve thinking about questions such as "*where did I come from?*" and "*why am I here?*" — questions that are difficult to find answers to.
2) A spiritual person might also be described as someone who's more aware of things that aren't simply physical — they feel there's another dimension to life.
3) It's about feelings of awe and wonder, or a sense of inner peace. Some people might get these kinds of feeling from a beautiful sunset, a wild sea or a rugged mountain range.
4) Spirituality could also be described as being self-aware — aware of your actions and their effects on others, or having a deeper understanding of your self-worth or purpose in life.
5) This might lead to a more refined recognition of the value of the world, of our place within it, and of those we share the planet with. A less selfish world-view perhaps.

6) For religious believers, spirituality is linked strongly to their beliefs in God. Others say that although they don't believe in God as such, and don't belong to a specific faith, they do believe in 'something'.

There are Different Ways of Expressing Spirituality

1) Many ways of expressing spirituality are religious, but certainly not all of them.
2) Religious symbolism can express spirituality, like an ichthus (Christian fish symbol) on the back of your car, or a kippah (a small round cap worn by Jewish men). Your actions might also demonstrate spirituality — e.g. meditating, praying, leading a disciplined life, or belonging to a faith community. A faith community can range from a monastic lifestyle to taking part in community-based activities.

Eating cake is not normally thought of as being particularly spiritual.

3) For those who have no specific faith, support or membership of a voluntary organisation (and the reasons for that support) would demonstrate spirituality.
4) But people can also explore their spirituality in a number of other ways. This could be through art, literature or music, or some other creative area. These activities allow people to explore their emotions in an attempt to produce work of beauty and meaning.

Spirituality — nothing to do with drinking gin...

Hmmm — a page about spirituality to get the book going. Not the easiest thing in the world to get your head round... but interesting. Just let me tell you one thing — you definitely shouldn't be put off by this 'heavy' opening page. This is a cracking subject, and a whole lot more interesting than maths. Read on...

General

The Nature of Truth

Quick — do French instead. No... okay, you have been warned. Well, a page about the 'Nature of Truth' it is then. But there are different kinds of truth. And they all have their problems. Yep, I know... tricky.

There are Four Main Kinds of Truth

1 Scientific Truth

This is what people often mean by 'truth'. Scientists test their theories by observing things or performing experiments. But even if the same thing happens every time, does that necessarily mean their theory is true... A more accurate measurement or sophisticated experiment might give a different result.

2 Historical Truth

We work out what happened in the past by looking at historical evidence (e.g. eyewitness accounts, archaeological evidence etc.). But an eyewitness account might be biased. And other kinds of evidence can be misinterpreted, so it's difficult to say for sure that we know what went on.

3 Moral Truth

A person's idea of moral truth is what they believe to be morally right or wrong. They might arrive at this conclusion through thinking about life, watching or talking to people, or perhaps through thinking about what their religion teaches. For example, one person might think, "*It's always wrong to lie,*" whereas another person might think, "*It's generally wrong to lie, but if a lie will stop someone getting hurt unnecessarily, then it's okay.*"

4 Spiritual Truth / Religious Truth

Two different Christians (for example) might interpret the Bible in different ways, and each could claim that their interpretation comes from God — their versions of the truth are different. This kind of truth is a matter of faith and conscience — it's not the kind of thing that can be proved. But does that mean it isn't true...

Many people believe it's impossible to find absolute truth — certainly none of these 4 kinds of truth is infallible.

Evidence isn't the same as Proof

1) Evidence is a reason to believe a theory, and the more evidence you have for something, the more likely it is to be true. And with enough evidence, you might be able to persuade someone that something is true.
2) But even if you could persuade people of something, does that make it true...
3) Also, people might interpret a piece of evidence in a different way — they may argue that the evidence actually points to something else being true.
4) Proof, on the other hand, is something which definitely shows truth and can't be disputed.

People Look for Religious Truth in Different Places

Religious people look in various places to find the 'truth' about the nature of God, or what God wants.

SACRED WRITINGS Believers most commonly look to sacred writings (e.g. the Bible, the Qur'an or the Torah) for religious truth. But some people will claim that the Bible should be interpreted to suit the times, whereas others argue that it's the Word of God and must be taken literally. Who can really know exactly what God intended...

RELIGIOUS LEADERS Religious people may also look to religious leaders (e.g. the Pope), institutions (e.g. the Church) or their religious traditions to find truth. But religious leaders are human, and humans have failings — do they really speak on behalf of God... The same goes for members of the Church — *present and past.* And the Church and its traditions were founded by humans — so the same argument could be used.

CONSCIENCE You might also believe that inner truth comes from your conscience — that little voice in your head telling you what's right or wrong. Some people argue that this is the voice of God. Others say that people's ideas of what's right and wrong depend on their personal circumstances — e.g. your parents or your environment could influence what you think is morally right.

Everything on this page is true — trust me...

Yep — that was always going to be a tricky page, so don't worry too much if you found that heavy going. Religion is a matter of faith — believers will believe certain things to be true regardless of whether there is any real hard evidence or not. That's the nature of the thing. Now go back and make sure you know the truth.

Believing in God

General

Millions of people across the world believe in some kind of divine being or 'god'. They believe for various reasons — for some people, it's based on personal religious experience, but for others it's more indirect. For many people, the fact that they're brought up in a religious environment leads to or supports belief in a god.

It Can Start with Your Upbringing or a Search for Meaning

1) If you were brought up by religious parents and your upbringing itself was based on religious teaching, it seems more likely that you would believe in a god. The same would apply if you grew up in a religious community where life was based on faith in one particular religion.
2) The presence of religion in the world may also have an influence. It could be that you are influenced by the good work that religion does in the world — whether it be for individuals, communities or those who are experiencing suffering.
3) You may also be drawn to the purpose and structure it provides — or simply to the desire to have something to believe in.
4) The search for meaning is a major reason for people becoming interested in a particular religion. People want to find answers or find out why life is as it is, and they might believe religion can help. Becoming a follower of God in this way is called conversion.
5) This desire to find out why we are here or why bad things happen in the world might also explain why some people move from one religion to another.

Someone Must Have Designed the Planet

1) Many people are convinced by what might be termed 'design' arguments. The idea here is that the intricate workings of the Universe (or of life) can't have come about by random chance. There must have been some kind of designer and this designer was God.
2) Isaac Newton's thumb theory (*because every thumb print is intricate and unique, there must be a God*) and William Paley's watchmaker theory (*you wouldn't think an intricate watch you found was made by chance — so why believe the world was*) are both design arguments.
3) Even Albert Einstein, one of the most prominent scientists of the twentieth century (and an agnostic), said: *"When I see all the glories of the cosmos, I can't help but believe that there is a divine hand behind it all."*
4) Einstein might have been talking about design, but this might also be interpreted as a reference to a 'numinous' experience — something which inspires awe and wonder at God's creation (see page 4).

5) Miracles and the power of prayer might also lead someone to believe in God, but these are directly religious reasons which we'll look at later.
6) However, some of the non-religious ideas about the origin of the world might lead some people to become agnostic (someone who believes it's impossible to know whether there's a god or not) or atheist (someone who rejects completely the idea of a divine being).
7) These ideas might include the theory of evolution (often called Darwinism) and the Big Bang theory (cosmology). (More about that on page 10.) Miracles can also be explained by using science and this too may convince some that there is no god.

Looks like the jury's still out on this one...

Phewee — nice controversial page... Basically, religion's a personal thing — Bob believes cos his mum does, Sam gazes at the stars at night and reckons there must be a god, and Al doesn't believe at all. Learn all these reasons for believing (or not) — you get marks for including them in your answers.

General

Religious Experiences

There are loads of ways people claim to experience God. These religious experiences allow people to 'know' God as he reveals himself to them. A key concern for nonbelievers, however, is whether the experiences are real. Some might claim they're just illusions brought on by religious hysteria or a desire to believe in something.

Revelation — God Reveals His Presence

God can reveal his presence in different ways...

1) NUMINOUS
This word describes an experience which inspires awe and wonder and might allow someone to feel God's presence. For example, a beautiful view or a butterfly's wing might convince you there must be a creator.

2) MIRACLES
Jesus was renowned for his miracles — amazing events which couldn't be explained by the laws of nature or science. People claim miracles still occur (miracles of healing at Lourdes, for example) and bring people to God. Miracles are said to show God's power and presence.

3) PRAYER
Revelation can also come in the form of prayer (a dialogue with God) — a person might feel that a prayer was answered (e.g. by an ill person being miraculously cured), or they might simply be filled with a sense of deep inner peace or wonder.

4) RELIGIOUS SCRIPTURE
People can read religious scripture (e.g. the Bible, the Qur'an or the Torah), and feel that the nature of God has been revealed.

5) CHARISMATIC PHENOMENA (or Charismatic Worship)
Following conversion, a Christian believer may claim to have been touched by the Holy Spirit (see page 6) and may demonstrate spiritual gifts. These range from singing, dancing, shaking or crying during worship to 'speaking in tongues' (unknown languages), having visions or prophesying (predicting the future).

6) SACRAMENTAL RITUAL (see page 62)
For example, Holy Communion is an act of sacramental worship. The bread and wine are believed to actually become Christ's body and blood in the Roman Catholic Church (called transubstantiation) and this reveals the presence of God.

7) MEDITATION
Focusing mental energies on God may bring about visions or voices. These could be inspired by prayer, reading scripture or fasting. It doesn't need to be in a place of worship — you can meditate anywhere.

Conversion refers to the first time a person becomes a follower of God (although it can also be used when someone changes their faith). They might say they've been 'saved' or 'born again'.

Revelation can be General (for Everyone) or Special (a Personal Visit)

General revelation refers to experiences which are available to everyone, including:
1) acts of nature, conscience and morality,
2) religious scripture,
3) the work of religious leaders.

Special revelation describes experiences of God revealing himself directly to an individual or to a select group, e.g.:
1) visions,
2) dreams,
3) prophecies.

1) Some religious believers would argue that general revelation is enough for us to know God, while others would say that God must reveal himself in a new, special way for each generation.
2) Many believers would argue that a balance of general and special revelation is required.

"I've got a revelation here for a Mr Smith..."

Revelations, eh... Wow. I mean, just imagine. It's just mind-blowing...

The Nature of God

General

What's God Like? — The Debate Continues...

The question of what God is like has occupied religious thinkers for hundreds of years. There are three main issues:

1) Is God a kind of 'person' or a kind of 'force'?
2) Is God within or outside the Universe?
3) Is there just one god or are there many gods?

None of these ideas are without problems, however, and many people would argue that God is actually a combination of them all.

Is God a 'Person'?

1) The term 'personal god' refers to God as a 'person' — albeit an almighty and divine person. God would be someone that supports and cares for us as a friend would, with human emotions like us. If this were the case, prayer would become part of our individual relationship — a 'conversation' with God.
2) The problem with this is that God is meant to be omnipresent (everywhere at once) — which poses the question of how a personal god can be everywhere at once.
3) The term 'impersonal god' refers to God as a concept, a force or an idea of goodness and light. The 'prime number' theory is often used to represent this idea of God — something that can't be divided or reduced.
4) The obvious problem here is how you can have a relationship with a force or an idea.

Where is God?

1) An 'immanent' God is a God who is in the world with us — a God who has taken an active role in the progress of human history and continues to do so.
2) The problem here is that an immanent God may appear small and fallible.
3) On the other hand, a 'transcendent' God is outside the world and doesn't directly act in human history.
4) This view of God makes him remote and separate from our experience on Earth. However, Christians who see God as transcendent might argue that it is they who do the work of God and that he is working through them.
5) Unfortunately, this definition is a bit too abstract for a lot of people to understand.
6) Religious believers (and Christians in particular) often try not to deal with extremes of any of these ideas, preferring instead to draw on different aspects for different occasions. Many would argue that God needs to be a blend of all of the above.

How Many Gods are There?

1) Monotheism is the idea of one God. This exists in Christianity, Judaism and Islam.
2) Polytheism is the belief in more than one god, e.g. in Classical Greek and Roman civilisations, and some forms of Hinduism.

Although Christianity is monotheistic, there is a belief that God is actually three in one (the Trinity — see p.6) — the Father, the Son (Jesus) and the Holy Spirit.

One for sorrow, two for joy... three for a girl... four for a boy...

This is seriously tricky stuff — and not just for Religious Studies. These questions have been worrying loads of people for ages. But, tricky or no, you have to understand all these arguments to do well in that GCSE.

Christianity & Judaism

Christian and Jewish Teaching on God

Judaism and Christianity say Similar Things about God...

1) As Christianity grew directly from Judaism, the basic concept of God is something the two faiths share.
2) The Judaeo-Christian God is usually seen as male (referred to as He or Father) although nowadays many religious believers would argue that this is simply because when these religions were founded society was male-dominated, and that God is actually neither male nor female.
3) Both faiths share the ideas that God is omnipotent (all-powerful), omnipresent (everywhere) and omniscient (all-knowing), that God is divine, supreme, totally good and totally perfect, and that God has given us free will.

However, many Jews and Christians believe that our lives are predestined — we control individual actions, but not the ultimate outcome of our lives.

...but There are Some Big Differences

4) The biggest difference is Christian belief in the Trinity. Jews never believed Christ was the Son of God.
5) Another key difference between Jewish and Christian teaching is that Jews are forbidden to draw or make images of God.

The Trinity is Explained Nicely in the Nicene Creed

no pun intended

1) The Christian idea of the Trinity is perhaps best expressed in the Nicene Creed:

"We believe in one God, the Father, the almighty, maker of heaven and earth... We believe in one Lord, Jesus Christ, the only son of God... Of one being with the Father... We believe in the Holy Spirit... The giver of life... Who proceeds from the Father and the Son..."

2) God the Father might be described as the transcendent part of God, the Son as the immanent and personal part, and the Holy Spirit the immanent yet impersonal (see page 5).
3) Similarly, Christians might describe the Father as the creator and judge, the Son (Jesus) as the human incarnation of God (and the Messiah, or saviour), and the Holy Spirit as the force of God — inspiring, guiding and comforting them.

See page 45 for more about this stuff.

The Jewish Shema Prayer Talks about Just One God

"Hear, O Israel: the Lord our God, the Lord is one." Deuteronomy 6:4

1) This passage is contained in the Shema — one of the most important prayers in Judaism. The Jewish God is, therefore, quite clearly seen as one.
2) Maimonides, a twelfth-century Jewish thinker, came up with a set of principles of Jewish faith. These principles contain many of Judaism's key teachings on God (see page 73).

Christianity says there's a Devil — Judaism says there Isn't

1) Judaism has no concept of a devil fighting against God and tempting people into doing evil deeds. It is believed that God created all — and that includes both good and evil.

Satan is mentioned in the Hebrew Bible (particularly in the Book of Job), but this concept isn't really a part of modern Judaism.

2) Some (but not all) Christians do believe in an evil, spiritual force known as the Devil or Satan who is working against God, bringing evil and suffering to humanity. E.g. in one of St Paul's letters to the Ephesians, he says:

"Put on the full armour of God, so that you can take your stand against the Devil's schemes." Ephesians 6:11

Jews and Christians — separated at (the) birth...

I know, it's a jam-packed page, but it's all important stuff. I won't waste your time with stuff you don't need to know. You should be able to close the book and write down a list of similarities and a list of differences.

Muslim Teaching on God

The Muslim name for God is Allah

1) For Muslims, God is called Allah — and the word 'Islam' can be translated as meaning 'submission' or 'surrender' to Allah.
2) According to Islamic teaching, Allah is the creator of everything.
3) He is referred to by ninety-nine names in the Qur'an — these names tell you what Muslims believe about Allah and his power. They include: Ar-Rahim — The Compassionate, Ar-Rahman — The Merciful, Ar-Aziz — The Almighty. He is also called The Provider, The Just, The Maintainer, The Hearer and The Real Truth.

"He is Allah, the One, Allah is Eternal and Absolute"

1) This passage is taken from Surah 112 and describes the basic principle that Allah is one. Islam is a monotheistic religion (see page 5) and this belief in the oneness or the unity of Allah (called Tawhid) is a fundamental principle of Islam.
2) The ninety-nine names sum up much of the nature of Allah. He is loving and compassionate, he is the creator and judge of all humans, and knows everything they do.
3) Allah cannot be thought of in human terms — he is the Supreme Being and has no equal.
4) To Muslims, Allah is both immanent and transcendent (see page 5). He is transcendent in that he is the power behind the Universe and is outside, above or beyond both his creation and time itself. His immanence is demonstrated in this passage: "*We created man and We know what his soul whispers to him, and We are nearer to him than his jugular vein.*" Surah 50:16 (In this passage 'We' refers to Allah and 'him' or 'his' refers to humankind.)

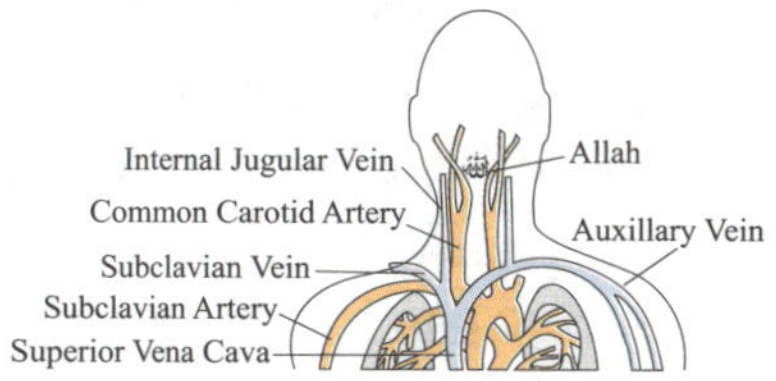

5) Human lives are predestined by Allah — but humans do have free will (see page 13).

There are Five Main Ways to Know Allah

1) Muslims believe that Allah has intervened in human history and that this is one way of knowing him and his power. His message was delivered by the prophets, of whom twenty-five are mentioned in the Qur'an. These include Musa (Moses) and 'Isa (Jesus). The last was the Prophet Muhammad, who brought Allah's message to the people.
2) Allah has also performed miracles.
3) The Five Pillars of Islam (see pages 95-96) also provide opportunities to know and be close to Allah. These are: Shahadah (a statement of belief), Salah (prayer), Zakah (charitable duty), Sawm (fasting), Hajj (pilgrimage).

Muslim prayer ritual — see page 95.

4) The Qur'an itself, being the word of Allah, allows humans to know him. Many Muslims learn it off by heart, and all try to live according to the guidelines found within it.
5) Allah is good and kind. However, there is a belief in a devil (called Iblis or Shaytan) who was cast out by Allah and tries to lead people away from him. Some Muslims would argue that Allah allows Shaytan to use this power to test and tempt us — we have the free will to resist.

Immanent AND transcendent? — I Qur'an't get my head round it...

There's some mind-boggling stuff in these last few pages about what (one or more) god(s) is/are. But at the end of the day, it seems Christians, Jews and Muslims all agree on the fundamentals — that God/Allah is divine, supreme, all-powerful and all-knowing, that our lives are predestined by him/her/it and that we have free will.

Christianity & general

Evil and Suffering

Loads of bad things happen in the world. People suffer from terrible illnesses and die in pain. Some people commit horrible crimes and other people suffer as a result. These issues often cause people to ask why. For religious people, the bigger question is: "*Why is God letting this happen?*"

Evil can be either Human-Made or Natural

Evil and suffering can be divided into two types:

HUMAN-MADE (OR MORAL) EVIL

1) This is when suffering is brought about by the cruel actions of people.
2) This includes things like murder, war, rape and torture.
3) The person causing the evil is able to make a choice about what is morally right or wrong.

NATURAL EVIL

1) This kind of evil, and the suffering that comes with it, is caused by the world in which we live and is no one's 'fault'.
2) This includes things like floods, earthquakes and hurricanes.
3) However, many recent natural disasters may have been caused by human interference in the natural world, raising the question of whether that makes those events human-made.

Evil can Lead People to Question their Faith

1) Evil and suffering may lead some people to question their belief in God — or even to reject their faith.
2) This might be because they can't believe that a God who is good would allow such things to happen, or because they feel that their prayers are not being answered (i.e. they think God could help, but doesn't).
3) Other people might argue that God can't be very powerful if he is unable to prevent suffering (i.e. God can't help, even if he wanted to).
4) People often argue that we can't know why there is suffering in the world — only God knows that. Suffering is often seen as a test of faith — God will have his reasons (even if we don't know what they are).
5) Praying for and helping those who suffer is often seen as a key part of various faiths.

Many people have tried to define evil and work out what it is or where it comes from. Some have argued that human-made evil is a psychological phenomenon that some people are more prone to than others.

The Christian View — Adam & Eve, Satan, a Test of Faith...

1) Christianity and Judaism teach that evil entered the world as a result of Adam and Eve giving in to temptation in the Garden of Eden — this switch from a perfect world to one containing evil is known as 'The Fall'.
2) After the Fall, every human being was born with a flawed nature — this is the idea of original sin.
3) Christians believe God created humans with free will — it's up to us to choose whether we perform evil deeds or not — just as it was up to Adam and Eve whether to give in to temptation or not.
4) Christianity has also personified evil as Satan or the Devil — a supernatural evil force over which we have no control. Satan was one of God's archangels but was thrown out of heaven.
5) Christians might refer to someone who has performed evil deeds as being possessed by the Devil, although this isn't really a part of modern Christian teaching.

oops...

Christianity and Judaism differ in that Christians believe Jesus was put on Earth to pay for the sins of all humankind.

Not the cheeriest page in the book, for sure...

Eeek — only 8 pages into the book and already we're into evil and suffering. Scary. You need to learn the distinction between human-made evil and natural evil, and the effect that any kind of evil can have on religious people and their faith. And if you're studying Christianity, learn those last 5 points as well.

Judaism and Islam — Evil and Suffering

The problem of evil, why people suffer, and how to deal with it. It's the sort of thing religion was invented for.

Islam and Judaism also say we have the Choice...

1) Both Islam and Judaism teach that humankind was created with free will.
2) Therefore, people can choose to follow God, or choose to do wrong.
3) Islam and Judaism also have similar perspectives on how to deal with suffering and evil.

Judaism says Suffering can have Positive Results

1) The Book of Job in the Hebrew Bible contains a key Jewish idea on evil and suffering. Job endures terrible suffering of all kinds and he questions God. In the end Job comes to the conclusion that God is all-powerful and knows what he is doing — and that suffering must be accepted because we can't really understand the world or God's plan.
2) Judaism teaches that we have free will and are able to choose what we do (like Adam and Eve — see page 8). But we are prone to making mistakes which could lead to suffering.
3) Like many Christians, Jews may also respond to suffering and evil through prayer.
4) The Jewish approach to suffering often stresses the idea that good can come out of terrible suffering. Suffering can bring people closer to each other and closer to God. It also allows people to make sacrifices for other people and draw on their inner strength.
5) The following passage is from taken from the Midrash (a collection of Rabbinical commentaries on the Tenakh or Jewish Bible): *"Not to have known suffering is not to be truly human."* It suggests that suffering is simply a part of the human experience and, therefore, must be accepted.

Although Satan isn't a part of modern Judaism, he does give Job a hard time.

The Qur'an says "Surely We Shall Test You"

1) Muslims believe that evil is a test of humanity's free will. Allah allows Shaytan (the Devil) to tempt humankind — we have free will so can choose whether to give in to temptation or not. It's a test of faith.
2) Islam teaches that if we choose to act against the will of Allah we will have to answer for that wrongdoing on the Day of Judgement.
3) The following passage is taken from Surah 2:155-6 — *"Surely We shall test you with something of fear and hunger, and loss of wealth and lives and crops... but give glad tidings to the steadfast who say when misfortune strikes: we are Allah's and to Him we are returning."*

This is remarkably similar to the moral of the Book of Job, when you think about it.

4) The idea here is that suffering should be accepted. Muslims believe that, despite suffering in this life, there will be joy in the next as Allah is compassionate.
5) Prayer is one way of coping with evil and suffering. If people pray for forgiveness when they have done wrong they will be forgiven. One of the ninety-nine names of Allah is Al-Ghaffar — The Forgiver (see page 7).
6) Muslims believe that those who are suffering should be treated compassionately by others. Many Muslims work to help those who are suffering.

"Will I be forgiven?" — "Best ask the Ghaffar"...

Three different religions, but pretty similar ideas about this stuff: 1) Suffering is mostly seen as a test from God/Allah. 2) You should always try to help others who are suffering. 3) Evil is wrong and against God/Allah, but if you pray for forgiveness after doing something wrong, God/Allah will be merciful and will forgive you.

Christianity, Judaism, Islam & general

The Origin of the World

No one saw exactly how the Earth came to be like it is... but science and religion still think they know.

Scientific Arguments — There are Two Main Types

COSMOLOGICAL THEORIES — How the Universe came into being

Chief amongst these is the Big Bang theory. Scientists argue that the Universe began in an explosion of matter and energy. Matter from this explosion eventually formed stars, planets and everything else. The universe still seems to be expanding today — important evidence for this theory.

EVOLUTIONARY THEORIES — How living things came to be like they are today

In 1859, Charles Darwin published 'On the Origin of the Species'. In this book he argued that all life on the planet originated from simple cells. Life evolved over millions of years into a huge variety of forms. According to this theory, we evolved from apes — not from Adam and Eve.

These theories are at odds with many religious arguments. However, if you don't take everything written in the Bible or the Torah literally, scientific and religious ideas can exist in harmony. Science tells us how, religion tells us why.

Religions have their own Ideas about all this...

Christian Ideas

1) Christian and Jewish ideas about Creation come from the same scriptures, and so are quite similar.
2) Christian thinking is based on the idea that God created everything. If the Bible is taken literally the process took six days, and humankind didn't evolve from apes but is descended from Adam and Eve.
3) However, if it's viewed as a symbolic description of a more gradual evolution, then it's possible to believe both in the Bible and science.
4) In 1996 the Roman Catholic Church accepted the Big Bang theory — definitely a significant acceptance of science.

For example, the Bible says things were created in the following order — the heavens (i.e. space) and Earth, the atmosphere, land and sea, and then plants, animals and people. This is pretty much the same order as scientists believe things appeared. So the timescale is different (millions of years rather than six days), but the general idea is the same.

Jewish Ideas

1) Orthodox Jews, who see the Torah as the word of God and so literally true, would find it difficult to accept scientific arguments about creation. God is believed to have created the world in six days. And humanity is believed to have started with Adam and Eve.
2) Progressive or Liberal Jews might argue that Creation as described in the Torah is more a way for us to understand, not an explanation of how it happened.

"In the beginning God created the heavens and the earth." Genesis 1:1

Islamic Ideas

1) Muslims believe that Allah created the world and everything in it.
2) However, unlike Christianity and Judaism, descriptions of creation in the Qur'an are not entirely at odds with science. Islam does not really have a problem competing with the Big Bang theory or Darwinism. In fact, scientific theories are supported by passages such as this.

"Have not those who disbelieve known that the heavens and the earth were of one piece, then We parted them, and We made every living thing of water?" Surah 21:31-2

In the beginning, God created Exams...

Albert Einstein once said that if you see something beautiful or amazing, you are seeing the work of God. Yeah, well... what did thicky Einstein know... But whether the Universe came to be this way through chance ('Big Bang') or design is a key question in the science versus religion debate. (See also page 3.)

Life After Death

Christianity & general

Every religion in the world has got something to say about death — and what they say can have quite an effect. What people believe will happen to them in death can influence the way they live their lives.

Life After Death — Some people Believe, Others don't

1) Some people believe that when you die, you're dead forever — that's it, your body will decay and you cease to exist.
2) Others believe that, although your body may die and decay, your soul can live on — in other words, you move on to a different kind of existence. This is the basic idea of life after death.
3) But it's not always easy to say exactly when someone's dead anyway. Are those on a life-support machine, who will probably never regain consciousness, really alive... It's not always easy...

Near-Death Experiences and the Paranormal

There are many reasons why people believe (or don't believe) in life after death.

1) Certain religions teach that we all move on to an afterlife of some kind. For some people, this will be enough to make them believe in life after death — they have faith in what their religion teaches.
2) Other people use the example of near-death experiences (NDEs) to argue that a soul exists after death. A near-death experience usually involves someone having an out-of-body experience when they are close to death. While apparently physically dead, they may have glimpsed what they believe to be an afterlife or Heaven, or spoken to long-dead family members.
3) Not everyone thinks of near-death experiences as proof of life after death. Some people believe that the visions are a result of chemical activity in the brain when it is short of oxygen.

4) The paranormal (things that science can't explain, e.g. ghosts) is sometimes used as evidence of life after death. Some people claim they can talk to the dead 'beyond the grave', and use this as proof of an afterlife.
5) Other people say that events we call paranormal have a scientific explanation — maybe we don't know what that explanation is yet, but there will be one. And some people don't believe that these events happen in the first place.

Christian Teaching — Heaven and Hell

1) Christianity teaches that the soul lives on after death (immortality of the soul). After death, your soul will go either to Heaven, or to Hell — depending on how you lived your life on Earth.
2) Heaven is often portrayed as a place of great beauty and serenity, a paradise where you will spend eternity with God — as long as you've lived a good life and followed the teachings of Jesus, that is. Those in Heaven are said to belong to the Communion of Saints.
3) Hell, on the other hand, is a place of torment and pain — the final destination of nonbelievers and those who have led bad lives.
4) However, not all Christians believe that these are real places — many Christians see Heaven and Hell as states of mind. In Heaven you'll be happy, and know God — in Hell you'll be unable to know God's love.
5) Some believe those who God finds unacceptable will be annihilated. They had no interest in spiritual things when they were alive, therefore their spirits were never awakened and cannot survive death.

And in Hell they make you wear bad wigs and false moustaches... forever.

6) Roman Catholics also believe in a place called Purgatory. Here sins are punished before the soul is able to move on to Heaven. This concept isn't in the Bible, so Protestants reject it.
7) Some Christians believe even those who led sinful lives may find salvation thanks to God's saving power.

Get ready to do some soul searching...

There are some complex moral questions to do with death. When is someone dead exactly... If someone could be kept alive by using a life-support machine but with minimal quality of life, would it be better to say they're incapable of independent life, and therefore dead... Dunno. It's one for your own conscience.

Judaism

Jewish Beliefs about Life After Death

It should come as no surprise at all to learn that Judaism has something to say about death as well.

Sheol — the Shadowy destination of the Dead

1) When the earliest Jewish scriptures were written, it was believed that after death everyone would go to a place called Sheol — where the dead lived as shadows.
2) Sheol was believed to be dark and damp, and your soul would stay there for eternity.

"Many of those that sleep in the dust will awake, some to eternal life, others to reproaches, to everlasting abhorrence." Daniel 12:2.

3) However, Jews later began to believe in an afterlife spent in places called Heaven and Hell — God would judge people after death, and send them to the place they deserved.
4) If you have lived a good life and performed worthy deeds, you will spend eternity with God in Heaven.
5) Those who have failed to lead good lives will go to Hell — a place of suffering and punishment.
6) Note that Judaism teaches that the body and soul stay together after death, and that Heaven and Hell are open to both Jews and non-Jews.

Your Behaviour during Your Life is Judged

"Our fathers sinned and are no more, and we bear their punishment." Lamentations 5:7.

1) Originally, there was a belief amongst Jews that you would be punished for the sins of parents or grandparents.
2) However, this view eventually changed and it was believed that it was how you lived your own life that mattered.

Three Kinds of Judaism means Three Different Views

Although most of these beliefs are held by all Jews, there are a few important differences between the different traditions.

Orthodox Jews believe that the physical body will be resurrected, intact, at the end of the Messianic Age.
Because of this, the body should not be cut after death (autopsies are frowned upon) and cremation is forbidden. A Jewish cemetery is called the 'House of Life' (Bet ha-Hayyim) and this also reaffirms the opinion that the body will be resurrected.

The Messianic Age is the period after the Messiah (the future leader of the Jewish people) is on Earth — Jews do not believe Jesus was the Messiah.

Liberal Jews believe that the body is simply a vessel for the soul, and it is the soul that will be judged by God. This is why some liberal Jews are now not so strongly against cremation.

Reform Jews are more concerned with the earthly life than with the afterlife. Their attitude is summed up by this phrase from a Reform prayer book: "*What can we know of death, we who cannot understand life.*"

See Page 76 for more about different Jewish traditions.

The Shadows — they used to be Cliff Richard's band...

Yep, in the old days, when Cliff Richard was a young rock 'n' roll singer (well before he started doing all that Christmas nonsense), he had a backing band called the Shadows. Now, an eternity spent listening to Cliff Richard songs isn't necessarily what early Jews had in mind when they came up with Sheol, but the thought of that would probably keep most people on the straight and narrow anyway. Scary as Hell, I reckon.

Muslim Beliefs about Life After Death

Islam

Islam, like other religions, has very definite teachings when it comes to life after death.

Akhirah — Life after Death

1) Muslims call life after death Akhirah — it's one of the key Islamic beliefs. Not to have a belief in life after death would make this life meaningless for a Muslim.

Only Allah knows why he tests us in these ways.

2) Islam teaches that nothing that happens to us during our earthly lives is accidental — Muslims believe we are being tested, and that the way we act in life will determine what happens to us after we die.
3) A key teaching of Islam is that we remain in the grave after death until the Day of Judgement (called Yawmuddin). On this day, Allah will judge everyone — not just Muslims.

Yawmuddin is the Day of Judgement

1) Although the earthly life is short compared with the eternal, Muslims believe it's still very important. It's in this life that Allah tests us. At Yawmuddin, it's too late to beg forgiveness for any wrongdoing.
2) Islam teaches we are judged on:
   i) our character,
   ii) our reactions to good and bad events in life,
   iii) our way of life.
3) Muslims believe everything is the will of Allah — so there's no point moaning about your circumstances. We cannot know why things happen, or what Allah wishes us to learn from it. The important thing is that we react to it the right way.
4) The reward for those who have followed Allah will be entry into Paradise — this is a place of peace, happiness and beauty. In fact, the Qur'an refers to Paradise as 'gardens of delight', filled with flowers and birdsong.
5) For those who don't believe in Allah, or have committed bad deeds, the reward is Jahannam (or Hell). The Qur'an describes Jahannam as a place of scorching fire, hot winds and black smoke. Here, those who have ignored Allah's teaching and failed to act righteously will be punished for eternity.
6) But Allah is also merciful, so many of those who have lived sinful lives may not be sent to Jahannam.

Allah is merciful and compassionate, but at the same time, he's a tough judge. Basically, if you're a good Muslim, you'll go to Paradise. But if you're a bad Muslim or a non-Muslim, you deserve Hell, but you might get lucky and be sent by Allah to Paradise if he's feeling merciful.

The Soul is the Real Person

1) Muslims believe human beings are Allah's greatest physical creation. They also believe that humans are different from other animals, because we know we will die.
2) Islam teaches that every soul (ruh) is unique and has free will.
3) At Yawmuddin, it is the soul that will be judged, as it is the soul that is our consciousness. Our body is thought of as a kind of 'vehicle for the soul'.

It's free will that makes human beings different from angels — angels obey him perfectly.

Muslims believe in predestination — Al-Qadar. Although we have free will, Islam teaches we cannot do everything we want — God is still in control. In recognition of this, Muslims will often say "insh' Allah" (if God is willing).

Stop moaning about your Exam — it is the will of Allah...

Yep, it's true. But a bit scary, all the same. I mean, if this is right, then since the day you were born you've been heading towards your own personal Day of Judgement — your RS Exam. And there's nothing you could have done to stop that. Not that you'd want to, of course. I was just saying, like...

Christianity & general

Life & Death and the Christian View

Abortion and contraception are subjects that people often hold very strong views about. And as you'd probably expect, religions have strong views about them too.

Abortion — Terminating a Pregnancy

1) Abortion is when a foetus is removed prematurely from the womb, before it is able to survive.
2) Abortion has been legal in England, Scotland and Wales since 1967. It can take place up till the 24th week of pregnancy, as long as two doctors agree that it's required. They must consider the quality of life of the woman, the unborn child, and any children the mother may already have.

There are complicated arguments for and against abortion...

i) The 'pro-choice' argument says that a woman has a right to choose what happens to her body (and since the foetus isn't independent of the woman, this argument says it must be considered part of the woman).
ii) But is it right to consider the foetus part of the mother when it's genetically different?
iii) Although many people are generally against abortion (seeing it as the taking of a life) they will agree that in certain circumstances, abortion should be permitted, e.g. if the mother's or child's health is at risk, if a woman has become pregnant through rape, or if a mother is too young to cope with a child.
iv) The question of when life actually begins is important here, too. Is it at conception (as the Roman Catholic Church says)? Or at birth? And is a foetus an actual person, or just a potential person?

3) Abortion is a very complicated and emotional issue, but generally speaking, Christianity teaches that abortion is undesirable. However, the Roman Catholic Church goes so far as to say that abortion is wrong.

"*Abortion has been considered murder since the first centuries of the Church, and nothing permits it to be considered otherwise.*" — Pope Paul VI (Leader of Roman Catholic Church, 1970)

4) Not all Christian churches see it in such 'black-and-white' terms, however. The Church of England believes that abortion is permissible in certain circumstances, while the Religious Society of Friends (the Quakers) argues that the life of the unborn child cannot be valued above that of the woman.
5) Indeed, many Christians argue that allowing a woman to choose is a way of showing Christian compassion — whether they agree with the choice made or not.

Contraception — Preventing a Pregnancy

1) Contraception (or birth control) is anything which aims to prevent a woman from becoming pregnant.
2) The Roman Catholic Church believes that preventing conception is against 'natural law'. Indeed, it teaches that humans have an obligation to 'be fruitful and increase in number'. Many individual Roman Catholics disagree with this.
3) The Anglican Church suggests that contraception allows parents to plan their family in a more responsible way.

The 'Sanctity of Life' Argument

Probably the most important biblical passage regarding the Sanctity of Life argument is the sixth of the Ten Commandments, "*You shall not murder.*" — Exodus 20:13

1) Because the Bible says we were created in the image of God and given the gift of life, many Christians believe that we do not have the right to interfere with when life ends, or to prevent the beginning of a new life.
2) Although the Bible doesn't actually mention abortion, other Christian writings (e.g. the Didache, a 2nd century manual of Christian teaching) are quite specifically against it.

It's tricky, emotional stuff...

There are no easy answers. So learn the stuff on the page, and be ready to give both sides of the argument.

Life & Death and the Christian View

Christianity & general

Another couple of very complicated subjects...

Euthanasia is often called Mercy Killing

Euthanasia means killing someone painlessly to relieve suffering, especially from an incurable illness. It's often called mercy killing.

1) There are two forms of euthanasia — voluntary euthanasia and involuntary euthanasia.
2) Voluntary euthanasia is when an ill person actively requests assistance to die, or refuses treatment which is keeping them alive, i.e. the person decides that they want to die and seeks help to achieve this.
3) Involuntary euthanasia is when the patient is unable to make such a request, and the decision is made by someone else — usually doctors and family members.
4) Suicide is when someone takes their own life — usually because of depression or illness. Attempted suicide used to be a crime in the UK, although it's now seen as a sign that someone needs help.

Euthanasia is Illegal in the UK

1) Euthanasia is illegal in the UK, but it is allowed in certain circumstances in the Netherlands and in parts of Australia, as long as two doctors agree.
2) Many people want euthanasia legalised in the UK. The Voluntary Euthanasia Society (EXIT) believes that many people would be grateful of 'the mercy of a painless death'.
3) Legalisation would mean that scarce medical resources could be saved for people who could be cured.
4) Many doctors have even admitted helping patients to die, sometimes by giving a patient an excess of painkillers, which ease suffering but can also lead to eventual death — this is known as 'double effect'.
5) However, there is a concern that if euthanasia were legalised, the elderly may feel under pressure to end their life, even if they don't want to.

Although unsure why exactly, Ed's Grandpa had a bad feeling about the offer of a holiday in the Netherlands.

"Your Body is a Temple of the Holy Spirit"

1) The passage in the subheading (from 1 Corinthians) suggests that God lives within each of us. Life is seen as a sacred gift, and so both euthanasia and suicide are seen as wrong by many Christians (see page 14 — the 'Sanctity of Life' argument).
2) Roman Catholics are the most strongly opposed to euthanasia. They believe that anything which intentionally causes death is 'a grave violation of the law of God'.

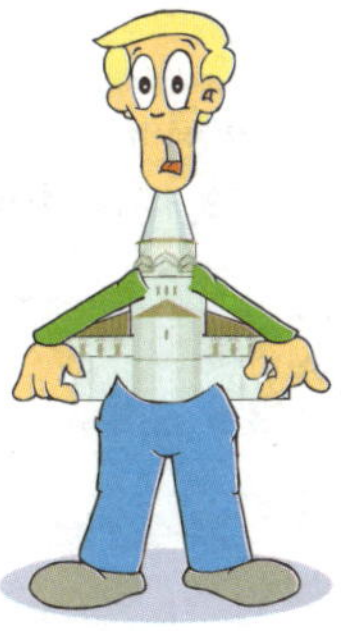

3) However, many Christians suggest that the easing of suffering is a way of demonstrating Christian compassion, and that the use of 'extraordinary treatment' (e.g. life-support machines) to keep a person alive is not always the best approach.
4) Most Anglican denominations agree that terrible distress should not be suffered at all costs, and that death may be considered a blessing. They argue that the quality of life must also be considered.
5) Local churches often have links with hospices. A hospice is a place where terminally ill people can be cared for, and can discuss any fears they may have about death.

I told you it was complicated...

Some syllabuses also need you to know about assisted suicide. Euthanasia and assisted suicide are pretty similar — it all depends on who performs the last act of someone's life. If a doctor gives a lethal injection, it's euthanasia. But if a patient takes a fatal dose of pills provided by a doctor, it's assisted suicide.

Life & Death in Judaism

There are no black and whites in any of this — only shades of grey...
But this is abortion and contraception we're dealing with.

Abortion and Contraception — Generally seen as Bad

> "Be fruitful and increase in number... fill the Earth." Genesis 1:28

> "There is no god besides me. I put to death and I bring to life" Deuteronomy 32:39

1) As a general rule, Judaism is opposed to abortion, contraception and euthanasia — the passages on the right are often used to support this view.
2) Judaism traditionally teaches that a child is a gift from God, and contraception interferes with God's plans to bless couples with children. However, most Jews are happy with the use of contraception for family planning, or if a woman could be physically or psychologically harmed by pregnancy. (Having said that, not wanting to have children isn't a good enough reason to use contraception for many Orthodox Jews.)

3) Sex should still be as natural as possible, though, so condoms are generally frowned upon. But their use may be encouraged by some as a means of preventing the spread of HIV and other STIs.

Sexually transmitted infections.

Be fruitful and multiply...

See page 14 for some more general arguments about abortion.

4) Abortion is generally seen by Jews as being worse than contraception, because a potential life is being denied existence. However, Judaism does not believe that the life of an unborn child is more valuable than that of the mother.
5) Many Jews accept that, in certain cases, abortion should be allowed. Some rabbis allow abortion if pregnancy becomes physically or mentally dangerous for the woman concerned, or if the child is likely to be severely disabled and unable to lead a full life. But it cannot simply be carried out for convenience.
6) The later in the pregnancy abortion is requested, the more difficult it becomes for Judaism to allow it.

Only God can Decide when we Die

1) Jewish teaching is, generally, opposed to the practice of euthanasia — life is seen as a gift from God and is therefore sacred. We do not have the right to decide when a life should end.
2) The same thing applies to suicide — it is seen as such a great sin that those who take their own lives are not buried in the same part of the cemetery as other Jews.
3) However, the relief of pain and suffering is a key part of Jewish teaching. So although euthanasia is seen as wrong if it involves actively doing something to cause someone's death, it may be possible to withhold treatment, if this treatment was causing further distress.
4) The words of Rabbi Moses Isserles are sometimes used to argue that it may be reasonable to switch off a life-support machine that's keeping someone alive.

> "If there is anything which causes a hindrance to the departure of the soul... then it is permissible to remove it."

Good lord — it's not like maths, is it...

I mean, in maths, things are true or false, right or wrong, black or white... But like I said, with this it's all shades of grey. And that makes it harder in the Exam, since you have to be aware of lots of different points of view on the same subject. But on the bright side, you don't need to know anything about algebra...

Life & Death in Islam

It's all very tricky...

Islam Teaches that Life is a Sacred Gift from Allah

1) Muslims believe that Allah created the world and everything in it. Our lives are sacred, and only Allah can decide when a life may end or when it may begin.
2) This means that abortion, contraception and euthanasia are all generally seen as wrong.
3) In Surah 3:145, the Qur'an says,
"*No soul can ever die except by Allah's leave — and at a term appointed.*"

Slay not your Children...

1) The passage on the right sums up Islamic teaching on both abortion and contraception. Neither is particularly welcomed, although there are circumstances in which such practices are permissible.

> "*Slay not your children... the slaying of them is a great sin.*" — Surah 17:31

2) When the mother's life is in danger, abortion is seen as lawful. The potential life in the womb is not as important as the actual life of the mother.
3) Some Muslim women argue that they should be free to choose what happens to their bodies. Those that disagree claim that in the Qur'an it says that unborn children will want to know why they were killed.
4) Muslims believe that conception is the will of Allah, so contraception is unwelcome (although Muhammad never forbade it). But if it is used, only 'reversible' methods are to be used — permanent sterilisation and vasectomies are frowned upon.

> "*He bestows male and female children... and He makes barren whom he wills.*" — Surah 42:49-50

Contraception is permitted if:

i) there's a threat to the mother's health,
ii) it could help a woman who already has children,
iii) there is a greater than average chance of the child being born with disabilities,
iv) the family is too poor to raise a child.

See page 14 for more general arguments about abortion.

Allah knows Why we Suffer...

Allah even has a plan for you, Norman Shuffleploppy.

1) Euthanasia is seen as wrong by most Muslims — because Allah gave us life, our lives are sacred.
2) Muslims believe that Allah has a plan for every living person — he has decided how long each of us will live on this Earth and we do not have the right to interfere with that plan.
3) Islam teaches that life on Earth is a test. Allah knows why we suffer, and we do not have good reason to end our own lives, no matter how bad that suffering becomes.
4) Instead, those who are suffering should turn to Allah, pray and 'patiently persevere' — Allah is merciful, and all will be revealed on the Day of Judgement.

Religious Studies revision — it's a matter of life and death...

People interpret their religion's teachings in different ways, so it's difficult to give a clear-cut overview of what a religion teaches. The best you can do is usually to say that 'Some people believe...' or 'Many people believe...', but hardly ever, 'Every person believes...'. These are very 'human' topics, and people are very different. But giving the pros and cons about various issues makes for plenty to say in the Exam.

Christianity, Judaism, Islam & general

Fertility Treatment

There are many similarities in the opinions of Christians, Muslims and Jews towards fertility treatment. All believe that a child is a gift, and therefore all allow some methods of fertility treatment.

Infertility means an Inability to Conceive a Child

Nowadays, there are various kinds of fertility treatment that can be used to help.

Artificial Insemination by the Husband (*AIH*) — sperm from the husband is injected into the wife's ovum.
Artificial Insemination by Donor (*AID*) — sperm from a sperm bank (i.e. an anonymous donor) is used.
In Vitro Fertilisation (*IVF*) — eggs are fertilised in a test tube and (up to 3) implanted in the mother's womb.
Egg Donation — where an egg from a different woman is used.

In Britain, any extra embryos can legally be used in experiments until they are 14 days old — at this time they must be destroyed.

Christianity sees Children as a Blessing from God

1) Most Christian Churches believe that it's okay for science to assist childless couples to conceive — as long as the process doesn't involve anyone else.
2) For this reason, artificial insemination using the husband's sperm (AIH) is permissible. The couple can be blessed with a child — and as no 'third party' is involved, the sanctity of marriage is not interfered with.
3) Artificial insemination using donated sperm (AID) is a less favourable method in the eyes of the Church, as the sperm is not that of the husband.
4) The Roman Catholic Church is particularly opposed to IVF, as it can lead to the creation of 'spare' embryos. These can be used for experimentation or simply thrown away. Many Catholics argue that life begins at fertilisation, and that even an embryo has rights.

Muslim Views are along the Same Lines

1) Again, scientific methods are permissible — as long as no 'third party' is involved, and all other natural methods of conceiving have failed.
2) AIH and IVF are both believed to be reasonable, as the sperm of the husband is used.
3) However, AID is not acceptable as the sperm is donated. Many Muslims see this as a sin comparable with adultery, as the woman has become pregnant using the sperm of a man other than her husband.
4) There are also concerns about diseases that may be inherited from an anonymous donor.

Jewish Attitudes are Similar too

1) In Jewish teaching, there's an emphasis on having a family.

"Be fruitful and increase in number... fill the Earth." Genesis 1:28

2) Because of this, it's left to individual married couples to decide whether they need to turn to scientific methods of conception.
3) A Jewish couple might seek advice on the matter from their rabbi (religious leader).
4) AIH is usually permitted, but not AID, as the use of donated sperm might be seen as a form of adultery.
5) IVF is generally approved of — as long as the egg and the sperm are from the married couple involved.
6) Egg donation is seen as okay, though the couple will often prefer the egg to come from a Jewish woman.

Putting fertiliser on it won't help...

Not being able to have children can be heartbreaking for a couple. If the technology exists to have a child, but their religion is against using it, what should they do... tricky. If you know people with personal experience in this area, you could use that in the exam to put the religious view in perspective.

Revision Summary

Whoa... that wasn't such an easy start to a book. But, be honest, it makes you think doesn't it... Is there a God... What is God like... Why is there suffering in the world... It's not maths, is it. You might have your own views on all this stuff, but you won't get far in the Exam if you don't know some of the major religious teachings as well. So try these questions, and if you get any wrong, go back and have another look at the section. Then try the questions again until you can do them all without making any mistakes.

1) Explain what is meant by spirituality.
2) Give 3 examples of what might make a person appear 'spiritual'.
3) Describe some other ways in which spirituality may be expressed.
4) Describe 4 different types of 'truth'.
5) What is difference between evidence and proof?
6) What might religious believers use to demonstrate their particular religious truths? Describe any problems with this.
7) Explain how a religious upbringing can lead to a belief in God.
8) Explain one of the 'design' arguments, and how they might lead people to believe in God.
9) Define the following terms: a) agnostic, b) atheist.
10) What is meant by a 'numinous experience'? What other forms can revelation take?
11) What is the difference between general and special revelation?
12) Why do some Christians find it difficult to believe in an impersonal God?
13) Describe the main differences between an immanent and a transcendent view of God.
14) Explain how the idea of the Trinity allows Christians to experience every aspect of God (immanent, transcendent, personal and impersonal).
15) What do the words 'omnipresent', 'omnipotent' and 'omniscient' mean?
16) How do Jewish teachings about God differ from those of Christianity?
17) Explain the Islamic belief that Allah is both transcendent and immanent.
18) What is the difference between moral and natural evil?
19) Why might the existence of evil and suffering lead some people to lose faith in God?
20) What is the Muslim view on suffering?
21) Explain the most widely accepted scientific theories about: a) the origin of the universe, and b) how living things came to be like they are today.
22) Christians interpret the Biblical Creation story in different ways. Explain these different interpretations.
23) What do the Islamic and Jewish faiths teach about the origins of the world and humanity?
24) Describe two phenomena some people might use as evidence for the existence of an afterlife.
25) Explain what Christianity teaches about the afterlife.
26) What do Jews believe happens to people after they die?
27) How do Orthodox and Liberal Jews differ on their beliefs about life after death?
28) How might Muslims' belief in Akhirah affect the way they try to live their lives? What does 'Yawmuddin' mean to a Muslim?
29) Describe different views Christians may have about abortion.
30) Explain what is meant by euthanasia.
31) What is the difference between voluntary and involuntary euthanasia? And assisted suicide?
32) Explain the differences between the Roman Catholic and Anglican teachings on euthanasia.
33) Describe Jewish teaching on abortion and contraception.
34) Describe some of the circumstances in which abortion might be seen as permissible in Islam, Judaism and Christianity.
35) Why does Islam believe euthanasia to be wrong?
36) What is the difference between IVF and AID, and why might religious believers argue that one is permissible and the other not?

Christianity

Marriage in Christianity

Marriage — a pretty big thing in anyone's life. Including yours if you get a question about it in the Exam.

Marriage in the UK — Times are Changing

1) The number of marriages in the UK has been decreasing for at least thirty years.
2) At the same time, it's become more popular (and acceptable) for couples to cohabit (i.e. live together) — either instead of getting married, or as a 'trial marriage' before doing it for real. (However, government statistics seem to show that a marriage is more likely to break down if the couple lived together first.)
3) Despite fewer weddings taking place, 90% of women and 80% of men are still married by the age of 30. But there are also signs that things are changing, and that marriage is becoming more popular again.

Christians say Marriage Should be Forever

1) The Christian faith values marriage very highly — the joining of husband and wife in holy matrimony reflects the union of Jesus with his followers.
2) Jesus taught that marriage should be a lifelong union — marriage is seen as a covenant or contract between 2 people, involving commitment and responsibility. Christianity teaches that the purpose of marriage is for two people to offer mutual support and have children.
3) But the Church recognises that not everyone is called to marriage, and from these people it demands celibacy.

"...a man will leave his father and mother and be united with his wife, and the two will become one flesh." Mark 10:7

"You shall not commit adultery." Exodus 20:14

In Ephesians 5:21-33, wives are encouraged to submit to their husbands, and husbands to love their wives, laying down their lives for them as Christ laid down his.

BIBLICAL TEACHING ON MARRIAGE

1) Marriage must be faithful.
2) Marriage must be worked at — you have to keep on forgiving.
3) Marriage reflects Christ's love for his followers, and involves submission.

Sex and Marriage

1) The Christian Church teaches that the total giving of self in sex shouldn't be treated casually — self-control and sexual restraint are considered important.
2) Christians are urged to keep sex within marriage for positive reasons more than negative ones — marriage is believed to give sex a special status.

A Christian Wedding has Legal, Social and Religious Features

Most Christian weddings take place in church. The details will vary according to tradition and denomination, but all combine legal, social and religious features.

1. Hymns
2. Opening Statement (saying what marriage is about)
3. Declaration (couple and witnesses must state there is no reason why the couple can't marry)
4. Vows
5. Giving of ring(s)
6. Proclamation (that the couple are now married)
7. Prayers (and usually a sermon)
8. Signing of the register (to make it legal)
9. Closing worship

In an Orthodox wedding, crowns are placed on the heads of the bride and groom.

A Roman Catholic wedding will also include nuptial mass.

Don't let all this trouble and strife get you down...

My brother got married on a big fancy boat on the Mississippi. That's not very relevant, is it? So anyway, my advice to you is learn everything on this page about Christian teachings on marriage. Then go and watch Four Weddings and a Funeral while you're in the mood. Go on, it's a great film... vintage Grant... Ah, go on...

The Christian Church and Divorce

Christianity

Times change, and the old 'married with 2 kids' kind of family isn't as common as it used to be.

Family Life in the UK is Changing

1) There used to be 2 basic types of family that 'society' and the Christian Church considered 'ideal' — the nuclear family, and the extended family.
2) A nuclear family consists of parents and children. An extended family is where three or more generations live together or as close neighbours.
3) In reality, families can have very different structures — e.g. single-parent families and reconstituted families (where divorcees remarry, or find new partners).
4) Family life is changing in the UK — and one of the most important changes in the past 30 years has been the growth of single-parent (or 'lone-parent') families. This is partly due to more children now being born outside marriage, but it's also because 1 in 3 marriages now end in divorce.

Christian Churches have Different Attitudes to Divorce

1) Family life is seen as very important by most Christians — it's believed to be better for a child to have a father and a mother present (ideally the child's biological parents), so that he or she grows up with one role model of each sex.
2) Ideally, a stable family can give a child a sense of identity, a feeling of security, teach him or her how to behave in different social situations, and how to give and receive love.
3) The breakdown of a marriage is seen by all Christians as a tragedy. However not all Christians agree about whether divorce is permissible, or even possible.

The Roman Catholic Church states that it is actually impossible to divorce. Marriage is a sacrament — God has made the couple into one flesh, and this cannot be undone. However, a marriage can be annulled — annulment means that it was never a true marriage in the first place. This can happen if:

i) either partner did not consent to the marriage or didn't understand what marriage is about,

ii) the couple didn't or couldn't have sex, or one partner refused to have children.

Nonconformist Churches (e.g. Baptists and Methodists) will generally remarry divorcees, but an individual minister can refuse to do so if this goes against his or her own conscience.

The Church of England says that divorce is acceptable, but that divorced people can only remarry in church if they can find a minister willing to marry them. This doesn't satisfy every member of the Church of England.

Jesus talked about Divorce in the Gospels

There are different attitudes to divorce among Christians — maybe because Jesus himself was anti-divorce, but pro-forgiveness.

1) *In Mark 10:2-12 Jesus says that Moses allowed divorce because of people's 'hardness of heart'. But he says that at the Creation of mankind marriages were meant to last for life, and if a divorcee remarries it's the same as committing adultery.*

2) *Matthew 5:31-32 and 19:8-9 say the same thing — except that divorce is permitted to someone whose partner has already been unfaithful.*

3) *In John 8:1-11, Jesus freely forgives a woman caught in the act of adultery. But he tells her, 'Go, and do not sin again'.*

Ours is a nuclear family — we're always at war...

One of the things you mustn't do with a 'Perspectives' question is just rant on and on, giving your own personal opinions and nothing else. You need to know what the different religions teach about the various moral issues, and why. And a bit of 'background' (e.g. how family life is changing) is dead useful too.

Judaism

Marriage in Judaism

Traditionally all Jews have been expected to marry and have at least 2 children — a boy and a girl.

Marriage Matters in Judaism

1) To Jews, marriage is an emotional, intellectual and spiritual union. It is seen as the proper context for sex (which is seen as natural and God-given), but is also for companionship.
2) Family life is also important, as it's through the family that the Jewish religion and customs are passed on.
3) It's the Jewish custom for parents to arrange for their children to meet suitable partners. To help in this it was common to use a 'shadchan', or matchmaker (and it still is among the ultra-Orthodox).
4) Although 40% of UK Jews 'marry out' (i.e. marry non-Jews), those who take their religion seriously find this worrying — children of 'mixed marriages' are less likely to be brought up as observant Jews. Many Jews see this as a threat to Judaism's survival, and even a 'posthumous victory to Hitler' (see page 75).

Nowadays there are shadchan services available via the Internet.

Kiddushin — the Marriage Ceremony

Different Jewish communities celebrate marriage in different ways, but there are some common features.

1) The groom gives the bride a valuable object, usually a ring.
2) The ketubah (marriage contract) is read out. This sets out the woman's right to be cared for by her husband. The text dates back to the 2nd century BCE.
3) There must be at least 2 eligible witnesses to observe the ceremony.
4) The ceremony takes place beneath a huppah (or chuppah), a wedding canopy — this is a piece of cloth supported by 4 poles. It is thought the cloth represents privacy, and the open sides hospitality.

5) Blessings are said over the couple — normally by a rabbi, who usually conducts the service.
6) The groom breaks a glass with his foot in memory of the destruction of the Temple in 70 CE (see page 72). It's said that there can never be complete joy for the Jewish people until the Temple is restored — this is why it's remembered.
7) After the service there will be a festive meal and dancing, and shouts of 'mazel tov!' (good luck, best wishes). Among some Orthodox Jews, the men and women dance separately.

Divorce is a Last Resort

1) Adultery is specifically forbidden in the 7th Commandment — it's regarded as the betrayal of a covenant.
2) Judaism does allow for divorce ('get' in Hebrew) — but only as a very last resort after all attempts at reconciliation have failed. A woman cannot initiate divorce, but a divorce does require the wife's consent.
3) In Reform synagogues, if the husband will not grant his wife a 'get', the Bet Din (Jewish court) can do so, freeing her to remarry. In Orthodox synagogues, women who want a divorce but whose husbands will not grant one are known as 'agunot' — chained women.

Go on, learn it all — and I'll give you a Scooby-snack...

Rrrokay... Christian, Jewish and Muslim teachings about marriage and morality have a lot in common. This isn't so surprising — all three religions share the same Near Eastern background. And can I just say how nice it is to have a few happy pages after some of the previous ones in this section. (Apart from the divorce bits, that is.)

Marriage in Islam

Islam

Marriage is very important in Islam. Muslims are advised to marry, and Muhammad himself was married.

Marriage is Recommended for 4 Reasons

1) The sexual instinct is very strong and needs to be carefully channelled.
2) Marriage provides companionship.
3) Marriage provides a secure environment for bringing up children as practising Muslims.
4) A stable family life teaches us all to be kind, considerate and affectionate towards others.

"Whoever is able to marry, let him marry, for this will keep him chaste." — Bukhari Hadith 30:10

See page 24 for more about marriage in Islam.

"He created for you mates that you might find rest in them, and He ordained between you love and mercy." — Surah 30:21

Choosing a Partner is often your Parents' Responsibility

Practising Muslims generally want their children to marry other Muslims. Islam affects a Muslim's whole life, and being married to a non-Muslim could create tension, especially with bringing up children.

1) Most Muslims believe it's unwise for young men and women to mix freely, and 'dating' is discouraged or even forbidden.
2) In most Muslim communities, parents search for suitable partners for their children — i.e. Muslims often have 'arranged marriages'.
3) However, as marriage is a contract, both partners must consent to it.
4) Parents also have a responsibility to help if the marriage begins to go wrong.

The Marriage Ceremony — Customs Vary

The marriage ceremony is different in different Islamic cultures, but there's always a religious ceremony (witnessed by Allah) and a public one (witnessed by the community). They usually go like this...

1) A nikah (contract) is drawn up in advance by the families of the bride and groom, and a mahr (dowry) paid by the groom to the bride.
2) An imam (leader of prayers) is often present (though this isn't compulsory).
3) Vows are exchanged, and a marriage declaration is made by each partner. A Hadith (saying) or a khutbah (speech) may also be said.
4) There will be a big feast afterwards, though the men and women may enjoy this separately.

Divorce is the Last Resort

1) Divorce is permitted, but only as a very last resort. If things aren't going well, an arbiter from each family should be appointed to try to sort things out. But if this fails, there can be divorce, and remarriage.
2) When the man says 'I divorce you' three times, the marriage is said to be over. However, there's often a period of three months after the first of these declarations. This allows time for reflection, and also to ensure that the woman is not pregnant.
3) A woman can divorce a man in this way (divorce 'by talaq') if it was written into her marriage contract. Otherwise she has to apply to a Shari'ah court for a divorce 'by 'kuhl'.

"Of all things permitted by law, divorce is the most hateful in the sight of Allah." — Muhammad

This kind of divorce isn't legal in the UK, as shari'ah law (see page 92) isn't part of the British legal system.

But I never said I wanted to study a foreign language...

There's quite a lot of Arabic words in these Islam sections — and they're in the syllabuses too, so you need to know 'em. The same goes for the sections on Judaism — they contain quite a bit of Hebrew. So although your RS teacher never told you what you were letting yourself in for, it's too late to complain now.

Christianity, Judaism, Islam & general

Religious Attitudes to Sex

Christianity, Islam and Judaism have all formulated laws concerned with sex. But this doesn't mean that religious people think there is anything wrong or dirty about having sex — quite the opposite.

Christianity, Islam and Judaism have a Lot in Common...

Christianity, Islam and Judaism have a good deal in common when it comes to sex.

1) Traditionally all 3 religions have believed that the only right context for sexual activity is within marriage.
2) But nowadays you find liberal Christians, Jews and Muslims who'll tell you that this belief is outdated.
3) 'Orthodox' members of all faiths say that certain moral principles never change, however.

> They might argue that when their scriptures were written, contraception was unreliable and the danger of unwanted pregnancy very great. This isn't the case nowadays, though, since modern methods are almost 100% effective.

4) All three religions teach that couples should wait until they are married before having sex. In fact, it's very important to most Muslims that people, especially girls, remain virgins until marriage.
5) Promiscuity (having many sexual partners) is seen as wrong in all three religions — in Christianity it's seen as dishonouring yourself.

...but they're Not Identical

1) Judaism and Christianity are monogamous religions — adultery is forbidden by the 7th Commandment.
2) Islam permits, but does not encourage, polygamy. A man may have up to four wives, but only if he can support them and treat them equally.

> Muhammad actually had nine wives during his lifetime — although not all at the same time.

Homosexuality — Scriptures say it's Wrong

Homosexuality means being attracted to members of the same sex.

1) It used to be illegal in the UK for men to be involved in homosexual activity. In 1967 it became legal for consenting couples, over 21, in private. The age of consent was later reduced to 18.
2) The scriptures of all 3 religions seem to say that homosexual sex is wrong — although the relevant passages are interpreted differently by some people.

> *"Because of this, God gave them over to shameful lusts. Even their women exchanged natural relations for unnatural ones. In the same way the men also abandoned natural relations with women, and were inflamed with lust for one another: males committed indecent acts with other men, and received in themselves the due penalty for their perversion."* — Romans 1:26-27

3) Some people (including some priests) argue that the scriptures were written against a very different cultural background from ours, so we cannot apply their standards today.
4) Christianity no longer condemns homosexuality, but it isn't seen as the ideal.
5) Since 'same-sex marriages' are not recognised in the UK, homosexual sex goes against Church teaching. Therefore many religious gays opt for celibacy — meaning they don't have sexual relationships.

Oranges are not the only fruit, but that's all you're allowed to eat, apparently...

Oooh, here we go again... courting controversy. Well, not really. Homosexuality is a subject that lots of people have strong feelings about — either for or against. But even if you strongly disagree with what a religion teaches, you still need to know what they teach, so you can argue against it. Capishe...

Children and the Church

Christianity, Judaism, & Islam

Practising members of all religions recognise the importance of passing on their faith to the next generation.

Respect your Parents... and your Kids

The scriptures of Christianity, Islam and Judaism all say how important respect and honour are.

"Honour your father and mother, so that you may live long in the land which the Lord your God is giving you." — Exodus 20:12 (the 5th Commandment)

Christian Old Testament (i.e. the Jewish Bible)

This verse shows that it is just as important for parents to respect their children as it is the other way round.

"Children, obey your parents in everything, for this pleases the Lord. Fathers, do not embitter your children, or they will become discouraged." — Colossians 3:20-21

Christian New Testament

"Be careful of your duty to Allah, and be fair and just to your children." — Bukhari Hadith

This Hadith was recorded by Bukhari. (A Hadith is an Islamic 'saying'.)

Parents and Children Should Look After Each Other

Parents must care for their children while their children are young. Children must care for their parents when their parents are old. That's pretty much how Christianity, Islam and Judaism all see it. Seems fair.

"Show kindness to your parents. If one or both of them attain old age, do not be rude to them or send them away, but speak to them a gracious word." — Surah 17:23

"If anyone does not provide for his relatives, especially his immediate family, he has denied the faith and is worse than an unbeliever." — 1 Timothy 5:8

Religions' Attitudes towards Newly Born Children

CHRISTIANITY

Evangelical Christians in particular stress this — and they use various expressions to describe it, such as 'being born again', 'being converted' etc.

1) According to the New Testament, you cannot be 'born a Christian'.
2) It's said that God has no grandchildren. In other words, you can't rely on your parents' faith — you have to find your own. And your parents can't force you to accept Christianity — it's your decision.

JUDAISM

1) Jews believe that if your mother is Jewish, you're Jewish — whether you like it or not.
2) However, practising Jews recognise the importance of encouraging their children to 'keep the faith'.

ISLAM

1) Muslims believe that everyone is born in submission to Allah.
2) They may walk away from Allah as a result of their upbringing, but this is not the way things were meant to be.
3) If someone embraces Islam later in life, he or she is said to be 'returning'.

Mum's the word — why does that mean keep quiet...

It just seems weird, 'cos my mum won't stop talking. Anyway... the three religions have a lot in common, but they have a lot of important differences too. If you know that (as well as everything else in this book, plus everything else your teachers have ever told you), then you ought to do well in your Exams. ☺

Christianity & general

Prejudice and Equality

The world we live in is full of people from different religious, racial and cultural backgrounds. And the way each religion deals with this is important, as it can help or hinder the building of communities.

Prejudice has Many Causes

It's worth being very clear about what a few words mean...

Justice	the principle of fairness — both legally and more generally.
Equality	being equal, and being treated equally.
Community	the people living in a certain place, or a group of people with the same religious or cultural characteristics.
Prejudice	prejudging something or someone with no good reason, or without full knowledge of a situation.
Discrimination	unjust treatment, often resulting from prejudice.

1) People are prejudiced in all sorts of ways. The main forms of prejudice you need to know about are those based on race, gender, religion, class, age, sexual orientation and disability.
2) Prejudice has many causes, and is often the product of early influences. It frequently comes about as a result of being influenced by widely held (yet inaccurate) beliefs of a particular community or family.
3) Although prejudice is usually born of ignorance, those who are prejudiced against a particular individual or group will often resist education and continue to discriminate.
4) Discrimination comes in many forms... Individuals may discriminate by being violent and abusive. Whole societies may discriminate by passing laws which prevent certain people from doing certain things.

The Bible has Plenty of 'Anti-Prejudice' Stories

For Christians, the Bible has plenty to say on the subject...

1) The idea of 'do unto others as you would have them do unto you' is a fundamental part of Christian teaching (sometimes called the 'Golden Rule'). See page 49 for more info.
2) Generally Christians believe that everyone was created equal by God, and so they try to avoid discrimination and promote equality. They look to the example of Jesus, who told stories about equality, and acted true to his own teaching by mixing with a variety of people himself.
3) Perhaps one of the most famous stories in the New Testament is the Parable of the Good Samaritan (Luke 10:25-37) where one man comes to the aid of another simply because he is suffering.
4) But there are plenty of other biblical stories preaching equal treatment for all — these two are from the New Testament.

The Parable of the Good Samaritan

A man is beaten up and left half-dead by robbers. A priest and a Levite walking down the road see him, but carry on walking. But a Samaritan (considered an enemy by the Jews) bandages the man, puts him on his donkey, takes him to an inn and sees that he is looked after.

"...there is no Greek or Jew... barbarian, Scythian, slave or free, but Christ is all, and is in all." Colossians 3:11

"My brothers... don't show favouritism. Suppose a man comes in wearing a gold ring and fine clothes, and a poor man in shabby clothes also comes in. If you show special attention to the man wearing fine clothes, but say to the poor man, 'Sit on the floor by my feet,' have you not become judges with evil thoughts?" James 2:1-4

5) And Deuteronomy (one of the Books of Law in the Old Testament) includes these...

"Do not take advantage of a hired man who is poor and needy." Deuteronomy 24:14

"Do not deprive the alien or the fatherless of justice." Deuteronomy 24:17

By the way, 'alien' means 'foreigner' here.

The Good Samaritan — what a nice bloke...

This is a serious issue that often makes it into the news. And it's one that you might have personal experience of perhaps — and if you do, you can use that experience to help answer your Exam question. But be careful not to just rant on about yourself — you'll need to refer to the religious teachings as well.

Race and Religion

Christianity & general

The United Kingdom is a multi-ethnic, multi-cultural society, and this leads to questions of how racial issues should be dealt with.

Racism is One Form of Prejudice

It's a sad fact that some people are prejudiced against anyone from a different cultural or religious background, or simply because of the colour of their skin.

1) There have been many instances of racial discrimination in the UK in recent years — usually as a result of ignorance, misunderstanding or segregation. At times these have culminated in rioting or murder.
2) Racism is often based on stereotypes — fixed and standardised images of people, which can be used to promote negative thoughts and actions.
3) The media has an important role to play. Television and newspapers can educate — or help fuel negative stereotypes (see pages 42 and 43).
4) At the present time in the UK, Asians suffer from racism and racist attacks more than any other ethnic group. This has led to further segregation and increased hostility.
5) The Race Relations Act makes it illegal to discriminate against anyone because of their race, colour, nationality, and so on. It also makes it illegal to publish anything that's likely to cause racial hatred.

Christian Churches are Against Racism — usually...

1) Leviticus 19:33-34 contains some basic teaching on the way people from different cultural backgrounds should be treated.

"When an alien lives with you in your land, do not ill-treat him... Love him as yourself." Leviticus 19:33-34

This story's actually about foreigners living in Israel, but Christians argue that it also applies to the modern world.

2) There's a story about Simon Peter in Acts that's also relevant.

Acts 10:1-35 tells a story about Simon Peter. He is told by God not to consider impure anything that God has made. So when a Roman soldier Cornelius sends for Peter, Peter goes willingly, even though it is against the law for Jews to associate with non-Jews. Peter says, *"...God does not show favouritism, but accepts men from every nation..."*

3) The parable of the Good Samaritan (see page 26) is an example of Christian teaching on the treatment of people from other cultures. The Samaritans were a mixed race who suffered a great deal of discrimination at the time Jesus told the story.
4) More recently, Dr George Carey (the former Archbishop of Canterbury) spoke about the fundamental Christian belief that racism is wrong, and that everyone is created in God's image.

"Racism has no part in the Christian Gospel... it contradicts our Lord's command... It solves no problems and creates nothing but hatred and fear." Dr George Carey

5) Although Christians generally work against racism and inequality, there have been occasions when this hasn't been the case. The most infamous example was the system of apartheid laws in South Africa.

The Dutch Reform Church of South Africa (DRC) believed that God had divided mankind into different races and made white people superior. This idea became law.

Trevor Huddleston (an English bishop working in South Africa) was appalled by this and struggled against it using nonviolent methods, e.g. political pressure and boycotts. He became President of the Anti-Apartheid Movement, and argued that apartheid was against God's will. Apartheid eventually came to an end in 1992.

Racism — still a big issue today, unfortunately...

This is topical stuff, and is certainly an emotive area. In the UK prejudice against Muslims has increased in recent years. This has led to further mistrust and calls for segregation from some, and an increased desire for tolerance and integration from others. Like all Perspectives topics, it's not supposed to be easy.

Christianity & general

Injustice and Protest

There are different kinds of discrimination. And many people and organisations have fought in their own ways against what they see as unfair treatment.

Sex Discrimination — also Illegal

Most societies have always been male dominated, and have only started to change relatively recently.

1) The Bible gives different messages on the subject of sex discrimination. In the New Testament, women are found among Jesus' followers and he treated them equally — remarkable for the time.
2) But this is taken from St Paul's letter to his young assistant Timothy:
3) In 1975 the Sex Discrimination Act was passed by Parliament. This made it illegal to discriminate against people on account of their sex — especially in the employment or education fields.

"I do not permit a woman to teach or to have authority over a man; she must be silent... For Adam was formed first, then Eve... it was the woman who was deceived and became a sinner... but women will be saved through childbearing." 1 Timothy 2:12-15

But in Galatians 3:28 St Paul writes, "There is no difference between... men and women; you are all one in union with Christ Jesus."

Many People have Fought against Prejudice

1) Christianity teaches that we are all born equal in the eyes of God.
2) Most Christians would, therefore, argue that we should avoid prejudice on the basis of race, gender, religion, age, disability, colour or class. The Bible has plenty of specific teaching on these matters.
3) There are many examples of individual Christians struggling against injustice — e.g. Dietrich Bonhoeffer, Archbishop Desmond Tutu, Bishop Trevor Huddleston, Oscar Romero, Martin Luther King...
4) There are also Christian organisations working against injustice, such as the *Catholic Association for Racial Justice*, and the *Church of England Race and Community Relations Committee*. Christians can also be found working for charities such as *Amnesty International*.

"From one human being he created all races on earth and made them live through the whole earth." Acts 17:26

"...loose the chains of oppression and untie the cords of the yoke, to set the oppressed free... then your light will break forth like the dawn..." Isaiah 58:6-10

Oscar Romero was Archbishop of El Salvador. He struggled against the authorities who were badly mistreating the people of his country and, in 1984, was murdered for speaking out.

See page 49 for more about Martin Luther King.

Dietrich Bonhoeffer was a German Christian who felt the Church had a duty to speak out against the Nazis' treatment of Jews. He later became actively involved in a conspiracy against Nazism. For this, he was hanged in a concentration camp.

Archbishop Desmond Tutu and Bishop Trevor Huddleston (see also page 27) were active in the struggle against apartheid in South Africa.

Amnesty International campaigns around the world to promote human rights — especially those of prisoners of conscience.

Prisoners of Conscience are Imprisoned for their Beliefs

1) Prisoners of conscience are those imprisoned for acting or speaking out against government policy.
2) They are usually found in countries where human rights are not valued and governments are unfair.

Father Thadeus Nyugen Van Ly, a Vietnamese Catholic priest, was sentenced to 15 years in prison in October 2001. It's believed that Father Ly is being held for peacefully expressing his view that people have a right to freedom of worship and expression. His views are not in line with the policy of the Vietnamese government, and his public speaking on these matters probably led to his arrest.

Galatians 101 — I thought Snow White was better...

We're starting to get onto some very serious topics now — prejudice, racism. These pages have got plenty for you to think about. Sure, you need to learn it all for the exam. But this kinda stuff you should know about anyway. It's really important. OK, lecture over.

Jewish Attitudes towards Equality

Judaism & Islam

Like Christianity and Islam, Judaism teaches that God created people equal.

The Hebrew Bible preaches Tolerance

Racism is disapproved of in Judaism. The Hebrew Bible (the Old Testament) has a lot to say on the matter.

1) The Book of Genesis suggests that all of humanity comes from the same source and is, therefore, equal before God.

"Adam named his wife Eve, because she would become the mother of all the living." Genesis 3:20

2) Other messages of tolerance can be found in Deuteronomy 23:7, and Leviticus 19:33-34 (see page 27).

"Do not abhor an Edomite, for he is your brother. Do not abhor an Egyptian, because you lived as an alien in his country." Deuteronomy 23:7

3) Deuteronomy 23 contains a discussion of who should be called 'the Lord's people'. This could be taken as meaning we should show tolerance for other nationalities. However, the same chapter does contain references to certain people or nations who should be excluded.
4) The Jewish people are sometimes called the 'chosen people'. This doesn't mean they think they're better than anyone else — simply that God gave them additional responsibilities.
5) The stories of Ruth and Jonah (both in the Hebrew Bible, i.e. the Old Testament) could also be used to promote social and racial harmony.

The Story of Jonah...

Jonah was told to preach to the people of Nineveh, who had upset God. When he preached God's message, the people of Nineveh were humble and repentant, which pleased God, and so God spared the city, upsetting Jonah. But God said he was right to spare the city, and that Jonah was wrong to be upset. The message is,
"If God can love and forgive, we should be able to live with others too."

Before he got to Nineveh, Jonah was eaten by a big fish and stayed there for 3 days.

And Isaiah 42:6 shows that God does not want the Jews to turn their backs on non-Jews.

The Story of Ruth...

Naomi and her husband leave Judah because of a famine — they end up in Moab. Naomi's sons marry Moab girls — but soon after, Naomi's husband and sons die. Ruth (one of Naomi's daughters-in-law) stays very loyal to her Israelite mother-in-law, and becomes devoted to God. This line eventually produces King David (see page 72).
The message is, *"Good things happen to those who are nice to people from other lands."*

"Male and female, he created them" — Genesis 1:27

1) The above passage is sometimes read as meaning that men and women are seen as equals before God, although different, and with different responsibilities. (God did create two different sexes after all, so he can't have wanted us all to be identical.)
2) Some people involved with the feminist movement (fighting for women's rights) argue that the expectation for women to become wives and mothers is unfair, and has hindered women's progress.
3) Judaism doesn't suggest that women should not be able to follow their chosen career. However, there is still a belief that motherhood is a privilege, and women should devote some of their life to it.
4) But there are definitely differences of opinion on this. Orthodox Jews (see page 76) aim to uphold many of the ancient Jewish traditions, and so would be more likely to suggest that women should remain at home as mothers and wives.
5) However, Reform Jews are willing to interpret traditional teachings so that they are, perhaps, more relevant to the modern age. For this reason they're less strict when it comes to the roles of men and women.

There are also rules governing synagogue worship. Usually ten men (called a minyan) are required for a service, and it is men who read from the Torah. Also, men and women usually have separate areas for prayer. Reform Jews don't accept all these rules, however — women can form a minyan, and even become rabbis.

I don't believe the Jonah story — it all sounds a bit fishy...

Jews have suffered from a great deal of racism and persecution over the years. By far the most extreme form of social injustice was the Holocaust (see page 75), when discrimination became government policy. It serves as a reminder to everyone of how much suffering can arise from racial hatred.

Islam

Muslim Attitudes towards Equality

Islam is truly international — with followers from many countries, and many ethnic and cultural backgrounds.

Islam says People are Created Equal, but not Identical

1) Islam teaches that all people were created by Allah, and were created equal (although not the same). He intended humanity to be created with differences. But this just means we're all individuals. Hurrah.

"And among His signs is the creation of the heavens and the earth, and the differences in your languages and colours." Surah 30:22

2) Muslims all over the world are united through the ummah — the community of Islam. The ummah consists of all Muslims, regardless of colour, nationality, tradition (i.e. Sunni or Shi'ite) and so on. This can help promote social harmony, as no one is excluded or discriminated against.

3) Hajj (pilgrimage to Makkah, see page 96) especially demonstrates equality. Those on pilgrimage all wear simple white garments, showing everyone's equal before Allah — wealth, status and colour don't matter.

4) The fact that all Muslims should pray five times a day at set times, and face Makkah whilst doing so, also demonstrates unity and equality. However, in a mosque, women and men must pray separately.

5) There's also a message of tolerance and equality in the last sermon given by Muhammad before his death. He was addressing Muslims, but many interpret the message as meaning that we should all live together in peace and harmony.

"You must live at peace with one another. Everyone must respect the rights and properties of their neighbours. There must be no rivalry or enmity among you." Hadith

6) Muhammad also warned against nationalism (i.e. fanatical devotion to a country): *"Nationalism means helping your people in unjust causes."* — Hadith

Muslims are more likely to be subjected to racially motivated attacks, abuse and murder than their white neighbours in the UK.

As a result a number of peaceful pressure groups have been established — some working within Muslim communities, others working with the Government or with other faith groups.

The Qur'an teaches that Men and Women are Equal

1) There's often a feeling amongst non-Muslims that women are treated poorly in Islam. However, the Qur'an says that Allah created men and women as equal but different:

"All people are equal...as the teeth of a comb. No Arab can claim merit over a non-Arab, nor a white over a black person, nor male over female." Hadith

2) Having said this, there are also some teachings which might be interpreted as meaning men are superior. Although what it actually means is that men and women just have different roles within the community or family — men are responsible for providing for the family, and women are responsible for the home.

"Men are the protectors and maintainers of women." Surah 4:34

For this reason, the Qur'an says a woman's inheritance need only be half as big as a man's.

3) However, there's nothing that prevents women from working. In fact, one of Muhammad's wives was a successful businesswoman.

4) Some believe that Muslim women who wear a veil (or Hijab) are being treated as second class — but many Muslim women would argue that it's a sign of modesty and allows them to go about their business without being seen simply as sex objects.

Equal but not the same — don't try that one in maths...

In Islam, a woman's traditional role has been to create a halal homelife where a family could be raised, while the man went out to work and made sure the children were good Muslims. However, that's not to say that all Muslims, no matter where they live, will live in this traditional way. It's more likely in some cultures that there will be complete equality between Muslim men and women — in education, religion and everything else.

Christianity and Other Religions

Christianity & general

Christianity is a very diverse faith, with many different denominations under the Christian umbrella. But that's not to say that it's always been particularly tolerant of other religions.

The UK is a Diverse, Multi-Faith Society

1) The United Kingdom is a very diverse, multi-faith society, and religious freedom is a legal right.
2) In most major towns and cities you will find a variety of places of worship — including different churches, synagogues and mosques.
3) Children in most UK schools are taught about all major world faiths in an attempt to increase understanding and tolerance.

Although some Roman Catholic and other church schools limit the amount of time spent looking at other religions.

4) Christianity is generally tolerant of other religions, both in the UK and globally. However, this hasn't always been the case.
5) In the past, Christians often believed they had the right to make people accept their faith as the only true way. Other religions were often seen as being primitive...

In the 19th century (when Britain ruled about a third of the world), Christianity was often forced upon other cultures.

In the crusades of the 11th, 12th and 13th centuries Christians attempted to reclaim the Holy Land from the Muslims. They believed that they were fighting a Holy or Just War against infidels (or unbelievers).

Christians believe Christianity is the Only True Faith

1) Christians generally believe that people have the right to practise any faith, although they might argue that only Christianity has the truth about God. This passage stresses the Christian belief that it is only through following the teachings of Jesus Christ that people can reach God.

"I am the way and the truth and the life. No one comes to the Father except through me." John 14:6

2) Some, however, abuse this idea and are less tolerant of other faiths.
3) The *New Catechism of the Roman Catholic Church* (a sort of religious instruction book) makes it clear that "*...the Church still has the obligation and also the sacred right to evangelise all men*".
4) 'Evangelise' means spread the Christian message with the aim of converting people to the faith. Many so-called evangelical preachers or evangelical churches base much of their work on this principle.

The ecumenical movement works within Christianity — it tries to create unity amongst the different Christian traditions (see also page 52).

5) There are also Christian missionaries who believe they have a mission to spread the message of Christianity and convert people.
6) Some of these approaches may be described as exclusive — they don't particularly welcome other faiths, and may even reject them because Christianity is seen as the only way.

Pluralists say there's Room for Everyone

1) Most Christians are happy to live alongside other faiths in the UK. Many Christian organisations (along with those from many other faiths) belong to 'The Inter Faith Network for the UK'.
2) The aim of this network is to promote mutual understanding and combat prejudice. This is an example of pluralism — the idea that there's room for everyone.

The Inter Faith Network for the UK describes itself as based "*...on the principle that dialogue and cooperation can only prosper if they are rooted in respectful relationships which do not blur or undermine the distinctiveness of different religious traditions*".

Pluralism — is that, like, being against more than one of something...

Exclusivism and inclusivism are also things you need to know about. Exclusivism is when a religion teaches that it is the only way to salvation. Inclusivism means the opposite — that salvation need not come through Christianity, say — other religions are 'just as good'. Ooh, it's a tricky subject, is this... make no mistake.

Judaism & Islam

Judaism, Islam and Other Religions

Islam, Christianity and Judaism have a great deal in common, and their approach to other religions is generally one of tolerance and mutual understanding. Over the years, however, there have been times of misunderstanding, ignorance, intolerance and prejudice which have led to discrimination and even war.

Jews believe Judaism is the Only True Faith (for Jews)

1) Judaism teaches that it is the only true faith for Jews to follow, but is tolerant of other faiths.
2) Most faiths have similar moral and spiritual laws and are, therefore, tolerated by Judaism. Because of this, there's no real desire to convert people.
3) People of any religion are generally deemed to be righteous if they follow the Noahide Code (seven moral laws given to Noah after the flood), or a similar spiritual path which guides them to God. And all righteous people will have a share in a world (or a new age) where humanity will be united under God.

> *"And so we wait for you O Lord our God... to establish the world under the kingship of the Almighty... when all human beings will call upon your name..."* from a Jewish prayer

4) Islam and Judaism have very similar beliefs in one God (they're both pure monotheistic religions — see page 5).
5) However, some Jews have difficulties with the Christian belief that Jesus Christ was the incarnation of God, and with the use of icons in Roman Catholic and Orthodox Christianity.
6) But there's still a great deal of mutual respect, and Jewish participation in interfaith groups (see page 31) is common. One example of an interfaith group is '*The Council for Christians and Jews*'.
7) It's sometimes suggested that Islam and Christianity grew from the same seed as Judaism, making the three faiths similar and creating a general air of understanding and tolerance.

Muslims believe Islam is the Only True Faith

1) It's said that Allah created all humanity from "*a single soul*" and "*made you into nations and tribes, that you may know each other, not that you may despise each other.*" Surah 49:13

> *"Those who believe in the Qur'an, and those who are Jews, and Christians — whoever believes in God and the Last Day and does right — surely their reward is with their Lord."* Surah 2:62

2) Islam believes that it is the only true faith — although there is an acceptance that all righteous people will be favoured by Allah, as he knows all we do.
3) Some Muslims (like some Christians and Jews) might interpret some of the words in the scriptures to argue that Islam should be exclusive, and should not have anything to do with other faiths.
4) Some Muslims may even feel that they have a mission to lead non-Muslims to Allah.
5) However, many Muslims in the UK live side by side with other religious believers, and some take part in interfaith groups.

E.g. The Centre for the Study of Islam and Christian-Muslim Relations.

6) It must be remembered that Muslims believe that men such as Adam, Nuh (Noah), Ibrahim (Abraham), Musa (Moses) and Isa (Jesus) were all Prophets of Allah. So the Torah and the Bible are also seen as holy scriptures which were revealed by Allah (albeit edited from their original form).

I know what you're thinking — this is a righteous page...

Christianity, Judaism and Islam have a lot in common — which comes as a shock to some people. But don't go getting the idea that these are the only three religions in the world. If you want to do another RS Exam after this one, there'll be plenty of other stuff to learn about. Hurrah! ... ... I said HURRAH! ... oh...

Revision Summary

You're right... there's some heavy stuff in this section. And some of it's very topical — many of the issues in this section make it onto the telly pretty frequently in one way or another. For sure, when it comes to the Exam, all this extra knowledge from the newspapers and the TV is useful. But there's no getting away from the fact that you also need to be able to at least present the religious viewpoints — even if it's only to say why you disagree with them. So try your hand at these questions. And keep trying them until you can get them all right without breaking into even the mildest of sweats.

1) Explain why most Christians value marriage so highly.
2) List any features which all Christian wedding ceremonies have in common.
3) Explain how the pattern of family life in the UK has changed in the past 30 years.
4) Outline the differing attitudes held by Christians towards divorce and remarriage.
5) Describe a Jewish wedding ceremony.
6) Explain Jewish teaching on divorce.
7) Give 4 reasons why marriage is considered the ideal in Islam. Describe a typical Muslim wedding.
8) Explain Islamic teaching on divorce.
9) What is the teaching of Christianity, Judaism and Islam towards: a) sex outside marriage, and b) homosexuality?
10) Explain the attitudes of Christianity, Judaism and Islam towards caring for members of the family.
11) Describe some of the major causes of prejudice.
12) Give a brief description of the Parable of the Good Samaritan.
13) How might the media be used to combat racism?
14) Describe Christian teaching on racism using examples from the Bible.
15) How does the Parable of the Good Samaritan demonstrate Jesus' compassion and tolerance?
16) Describe the role of the Dutch Reform Church of South Africa in the apartheid laws of South Africa.
17) Describe how Jesus treated his female followers.
18) St Paul seems to give two different messages about the role of women — describe what these are.
19) Describe how one Christian (or a Christian organisation) has fought against prejudice.
20) What is a prisoner of conscience?
21) Give examples from the Torah of Judaism teaching equality and tolerance.
22) How might the stories of Ruth and Jonah be used to demonstrate the Jewish approach to racial harmony?
23) How might an Orthodox and a Reform Jew differ in their attitude to the roles of men and women?
24) Explain ways in which Islam encourages equality and unity.
25) Describe Islamic teaching on the role of women.
26) Why might some Christians believe they have a 'mission' to convert people to Christianity?
27) What are the aims of interfaith organisations?
28) What is meant by: a) pluralism, b) exclusivism, c) inclusivism?
29) Why might Jews not feel that they need to convert people to Judaism?
30) Explain Islamic teaching on other religions.

Christianity & general

Christianity and Poverty

Poverty causes great suffering in the world. So its causes and effects are of great concern for Christians.

Poverty Occurs for a Number of Reasons

1) The Brandt Report in 1980 identified an imbalance between the developed and the developing worlds. The developed world contains around 25% of the world's population but around 80% of the wealth. Little has changed since 1980.
2) Causes of poverty in the Third World include population growth, war, and the sale of raw materials at low prices. In the UK causes range from unemployment and homelessness to gambling.
3) Although possessing wealth is not against Christian teaching, occupations which may bring suffering to others are disapproved of — e.g. working in the arms trade, sex industry, or gambling industry.

Christians have a Duty to Relieve Poverty

"Rich nations have a grave moral responsibility towards those which are unable to ensure the means of their development by themselves." from the Catechism of the Roman Catholic Church

1) All Christian denominations have become more concerned with a fairer distribution of wealth. A key question is whether wealth ultimately belongs to God, and should therefore be for the good of everyone.
2) Charity is an important part of Christianity, and a concern for Christians is whether or not they should be wealthy. Though Jesus spoke of giving up wealth to help the poor, being wealthy is not against Christian teaching. Indeed, the Church is an extremely rich institution — this is a worry for some believers.
3) The Church often becomes involved in debates about poverty. Recent discussions have focused on issues like the National Lottery and the minimum wage, and whether these contribute to suffering.
4) There's also the question of who should be responsible for the relief of poverty — does the Government have an obligation here, or should it be left to local communities or charities...
5) A number of Christian organisations exist to tackle poverty — both in the UK and on a global level. These include Christian Aid, CAFOD and Tearfund.

"...the love of money is a root of all kinds of evil." 1 Timothy 6:10

CAFOD: Catholic Agency For Overseas Development

The Example of Jesus

Christians believe they have a duty to care for other people and use many sources of authority to stress this. The Bible contains many passages demonstrating Jesus' compassion.

"The man with two tunics should share with him that has none, and the one who has food must do the same." Luke 3:11

"Go, sell everything you have and give to the poor, and you will have treasure in heaven." Mark 10:21

"I was hungry and you fed me, thirsty and you gave me a drink... whenever you did this for one of the least important brothers of mine you did it for me." Matthew 25:35-40

Luke 16:19-31, Luke 6:20-31, Matthew 6:19-21 and Amos 8:4-6 also contain teachings on poverty.

CASE STUDY — CHRISTIAN AID

Christian Aid was set up after World War II to help refugees. It now has over 40 member churches in the UK and Ireland, and works globally to relieve poverty. It raises money through donations, fund-raising and collections.

Most of Christian Aid's work is in development. Although they do contribute to emergency disaster relief, they believe the best way to help people is by '*helping them to help themselves*'. They set up projects in the Third World drawing on the skills of local people. This is seen as more dignified than receiving hand-outs.

Development projects set up by Christian Aid aim to help with problems such as poor sanitation, education and healthcare, as well as disease and population control. The organisation also aims to change government policy which adds to the suffering of the world's poor, e.g. through Third World debt relief, and fair-trade products.

Well I think exams are the root of all evil...

The basic message here is pretty simple, I think. And if you need to learn about a Christian organisation working to relieve poverty, Christian Aid is just an example. You choose one you're interested in.

Judaism, Islam and Poverty

Judaism & Islam

Islam and Judaism have similar views on poverty. Both believe it's our duty to look after those less fortunate than ourselves, and both expect people to give some of their income to the poor and needy.

Judaism says, "Do not be hardhearted or tightfisted..."

1) The above passage from Deuteronomy sums up Jewish teaching on poverty. Maimonides said that the best way to give was "*to help a person help themselves so that they may become* self-supporting".
2) There are two main ways of giving to charity — Tzedaka and Gemilut Hasadim:

TZEDAKA: Tzedaka is financial aid — even the poorest in society are expected to contribute 10% of their wealth. All wealth belongs to God, and not giving to the poor deprives them of what they're owed.

GEMILUT HASADIM: This refers to kind and compassionate actions towards those in need.

3) Many Jewish homes have collection boxes (called pushkes) in which money for charity can be placed. Children are encouraged to use these boxes — maybe donating some of their pocket money each week.
4) Although Judaism doesn't teach that everyone should try to be wealthy, it does suggest that extreme poverty will make others responsible for you, and that the love of wealth may turn you from God.
5) Unfairness and dishonesty in business is condemned — you're answerable to God for any wrongdoing.

EXAMPLES

i) There are a number of Jewish organisations working to raise money and promote kind actions. These include '*Jewish Care*' and '*Norwood Child Care*'.

ii) On a more global level is '*Tzedek*' — this charity, using the slogan '*Jewish care for a just world*', is concerned with things such as aid, debt relief, refugees and the environment.

The Islamic View is Very Similar

1) In Islam, the principle is much the same — greed and waste are frowned upon and possessions ultimately belong to Allah. Muslims are encouraged to act responsibly and help those in need.
2) Any work involving gambling, alcohol or anything sexually suggestive is forbidden, and moneylending is seen as immoral if those in debt are being exploited through the charging of interest. Some Islamic banks exist to get around this.

See also page 93 for more about Islamic living.

3) Again, there are two main ways to help the disadvantaged — Zakah and Sadaqah:

ZAKAH: This is one of the Five Pillars of Islam — 2.5% of your yearly savings should be given to the needy, no matter how rich or poor you are.

SADAQAH: This is additional aid — maybe financial donations or an act of compassion and love.

EXAMPLES

i) Muslims raise money for their local mosque which is then distributed to the poor.

ii) In addition, there are global charities such as '*Muslim Aid*' and '*Islamic Relief*'.

iii) '*The Red Crescent*' is the Islamic equivalent of the Red Cross, and the two often work together to bring aid to countries in times of war and famine.

It all sounds like good advice to me...

Both Islam and Judaism teach that we have a responsibility to the planet, its resources and our fellow man. We are stewards of the Earth and should not exploit what we have been given at the expense of others. It's a message that crops up in the 'environment' section as well. So I'd learn it pretty well, if I were you.

Christianity, Judaism, Islam & general

Religion and the Environment

Environmental problems today mean the Earth is suffering. Sadly, many of these problems are man-made...

Our Small Planet has some Big Problems

The environmental problems facing the world include...

i) Global warming (and the Greenhouse Effect),
ii) Deforestation,
iii) Extinction of animal and plant species,
iv) Pollution (leading to problems like acid rain),
v) Scarcity of natural resources.

1) Developed countries are the worst (but not the only) polluters. Competition means that businesses often feel forced to put profit before the welfare of the planet — if they don't, they may not survive.
2) Some governments look more to short-term benefits than long-term care for the planet. They may say they're trying to do the best for their people, and that people should be our first priority.
3) Governments in developing nations often claim that they're only doing now what richer countries did in the past, and that it's hypocritical for richer countries to tell them what they should be doing.

Religious Ideas about the Environment — 'Stewardship'

Christianity, Islam and Judaism have pretty similar ideas when it comes to looking after the Earth. All three religions teach that God has put us in charge of the Earth, but that we must do our duty responsibly.

CHRISTIANITY

1) Christians of all denominations believe that God gave us the Earth, but expects us to care for it — this idea is called 'stewardship'. We have no right to abuse God's creation — we must act responsibly.
2) There's pressure on governments and companies to sell goods and services, even at the expense of the environment. Although it can be difficult to balance taking care of the Earth with providing for humankind, this is what Christians believe we must try to do.
3) Christianity teaches that everything is interdependent (i.e. everything depends on everything else), so driving species of animal or plant to extinction, or harming the planet, eventually ends up harming us.
4) Christian organisations such as CAFOD, Christian Aid and Tearfund are concerned with putting this responsibility into practice. They put pressure on governments and industry to think more about how we are abusing the planet.

"We have a responsibility to create a balanced policy between consumption and conservation." Pope John Paul II, 1988

"The earth is the Lord's, and everything in it, the world and all who live in it;
for he founded it upon the seas and established it upon the waters." Psalms 24:1-2

"You made him [humankind] a little lower than the heavenly beings, and crowned him with glory and honour. You made him ruler over the works of your hands; you put everything under his feet:" Psalms 8:5-6

JUDAISM

1) Jews believe that we are the custodians of the Earth, and a concern for the natural world is often seen as being at the heart of Jewish teaching.
2) God's creations should remain as he intended, and we have no right to abuse them. Everything is interdependent, with trees being particularly important. Since the creation of Israel in 1948, millions of trees have been planted to aid the reclamation of the desert and help rebuild the nation.

"The Lord God took the man and put him in the Garden of Eden, to work it and take care of it." Genesis 2:15

ISLAM

1) Muslim teaching on environmental issues is very similar to that of Judaism.
2) At the Day of Judgement questions will be asked of us. We will be required to answer for any ill-treatment of the planet and its resources.
3) The Earth is seen as being a product of the love of Allah, so we should treat it with love.

Dr Abdullah Omar Nasseef stated at the 1996 World Wide Fund for Nature conference that, "His [Allah's] trustees are responsible for maintaining the unity of his creation, the integrity of the Earth, its flora and fauna, its wildlife and natural environment."

Look after the planet — or it's eternal damnation for you, my friend...

Once again, the ideas of all three of these religions are very similar. Which is good for me, since I don't have to write as much. And good for you, since you don't have to remember as much — even if you're studying all of these religions. If you're just studying one or two, then you've got it easy anyway, I reckon.

Religion and Animals

Christianity, Judaism, Islam & general

Religions usually say be nice to other people. But what about squirrels...

Christianity says Animals come Below People

According to the Bible, God created the world, mankind was created to populate it, and animals were created for the use of mankind. But animal-rights issues are still of interest to many Christians. For example...

- i) Animal experimentation (e.g. vivisection)
- ii) Factory farming,
- iii) Destruction of natural habitats (e.g. deforestation), leading to extinction,
- iv) Hunting,
- v) Genetic modification and cloning,
- vi) Zoos and circuses,
- vii) Vegetarianism.

"They [human beings] will have power over the fish, the birds and all the animals, domestic and wild, large and small." Genesis 1:26

1) One of the major issues for Christians is whether animals have souls or not. If they don't, then some people will argue that God created us as superior, and that animals are here for our use.
2) Christianity teaches that we should treat animals with kindness, but that they can be used to benefit mankind (as long as their suffering is considered). It's also thought that excessive money should not be 'wasted' on animals when human beings are suffering. So humans are very definitely 'on top', with animals below.
3) But some Christians point out that as everything is interdependent, our treatment of animals reflects on us. Indeed, the Church of England teaches that the medical and technological use of animals should be monitored 'in the light of ethical principles'.
4) The Roman Catholic Church is more likely to tolerate things like animal experimentation, but only if they bring benefit to mankind (e.g. if the experiments lead to the development of life-saving medicines).
5) Certain denominations are generally more opposed to the ill-treatment of animals — especially for our pleasure. For example, Quakers are particularly likely to frown upon zoos, animal circuses, hunting and the wearing of fur.
6) Unlike some other religions, there are no specific food laws to be followed in Christianity. So vegetarianism (not eating meat) and veganism (not eating or using any animal products) are a matter for individual Christians to decide about.

The Bible tells us that Jesus ate fish, and as a Jew he would have eaten meat at certain festivals.

Judaism and Islam have Similar Views

JUDAISM

1) The Noahide Laws (given to Noah after the Flood) clearly forbid cruelty to animals. Animals are here to help us, and not to be abused. And there are many stories in the Torah which demonstrate care for animals.
2) In Judaism, if meat is to be eaten, the animal must be slaughtered in a 'humane' fashion. This involves cutting the throat of the animal with a very sharp blade to bring about a quick death (see page 83).
3) Experiments on animals may be tolerated if they result in a benefit for mankind, but only as a last resort. Cruel sports are seen as an abuse of God's creatures.

Deuteronomy 5:14 says that animals deserve a day off on the Sabbath, just like people.

"I am putting you in charge of the fish, the birds and all the wild animals." Genesis 1:28

ISLAM

1) Khalifah is the idea that we're responsible for the Earth — Khalifah means Vice-Regent, or Trustee.
2) Cruelty to animals is forbidden, as is their use simply for our pleasure.
3) Muslims believe in demonstrating mercy and compassion for all living creatures, and animals used for meat must be slaughtered humanely.

"If someone kills a sparrow for sport, the sparrow will cry out on the Day of Judgement 'Oh Lord, that person killed me for nothing. He did not kill me for any useful purpose.'" Hadith

So it's OK to kill them as long as you eat them afterwards...

I bet you thought it would all be simple. You thought I was just going to say something like, 'all religions say be nice to furry things'. Well, they do — to an extent. But this is the page where animal experimentation and stuff comes in, which means benefits for people at the expense of animals. Which complicates things.

Christianity, Judaism, Islam & general

Religion and Crime

Christians believe that Jesus was forgiving and compassionate. Islam and Judaism also stress the importance of forgiveness and reconciliation, although the three religions do approach matters in slightly different ways.

Crime or Sin — State Law versus Religious Law

1) Most nations believe the rule of law is the best way of protecting people in society. Without law there would perhaps be chaos. With it, people know what they can and cannot do. The police enforce the laws of the land. The judiciary (i.e. the system of courts and judges) tries people suspected of committing a crime, and punishes those that are found guilty.
2) For Christians, there's a difference between a sin and a crime. A sin is when religious law is broken, i.e. when God's teaching is disobeyed. A crime is when the state laws are broken. The laws in the UK are fundamentally Christian, but are not actually religious.
3) Judaism teaches that Jews should obey the laws of the land they live in, as well as following the 613 mitzvot (religious laws or commandments) in the Torah.
4) Muslims have a clear and detailed religious law (shari'ah — see page 92), and this is often the basis for state law. Saudi Arabia, for example, is run according to this religious law.
5) All three faiths believe that God has commanded us to follow law.

For Christians: *"You must obey the authorities — not just because of God's punishment but also as a matter of conscience."* Romans 13:5

For Jews: *"You shall appoint judges...and they shall judge the people righteously."* Deuteronomy 16:18

Rabbinical courts (called Bet Din) exist in many countries to sort out Jewish disputes (see p 74).

Muslims believe that Allah sees all. He will know if you have committed a crime and you will be made to answer for it on the Day of Judgement. A truly repentant sinner, however, will be forgiven.

Punishment can have Various Aims

1) Most people believe that punishment should do some or all of the following:

1) deter criminals	3) protect society	5) help reform the offender
2) make the criminal pay	4) show the authority of law	6) provide retribution (revenge)

2) Punishment can take a variety of forms, including: community service, a fine, probation, a prison sentence, corporal punishment (inflicting pain, e.g. flogging or beating), and capital punishment (death).

CAPITAL PUNISHMENT

i) Many people say that capital punishment doesn't seem to deter criminals at all — most murders are committed in the heat of the moment (i.e. they're not premeditated), and in the case of terrorists, the death penalty might even encourage people as it makes the executed offender a martyr. (Also, there seem to be more murders in places that use the death penalty than in places where capital punishment isn't used.)
ii) There have been cases where someone has been proved innocent after having been put to death.

3) Many Christians are opposed to capital punishment, as it does not allow for reform — although some in the United States believe that it's a good thing. They say it protects the innocent and deters others.

The 'Howard League for Penal Reform' was set up by Christians to campaign for punishments that allow offenders to reform.

4) Judaism has allowed execution in certain circumstances, but only if there are witnesses.

"If anyone takes the life of a human being, he must be put to death." Leviticus 24:17

5) The same is true of Islam — in many Muslim countries people are executed for murder, or for speaking out against Islam. Also, adulterers can be flogged, and thieves can have hands cut off.

Crime and Punishment — wasn't that set in Russia...

Not for the first time, I'll say that this is a subject with lots of different shades of grey. Should we just lock people up and throw away the key... or is there something else we should be doing... Ho hum, well you should have known that you don't do RS for an easy life. No, sirree... that's why you have General Studies.

Christianity and War

Christianity

Although Christianity is generally 'anti-war', many denominations accept that a war can be 'just'. Individuals may not agree with this, however. They may be against war under any circumstances.

There are 5 Conditions for a Just War

Although Christians recognise that war goes against the teachings of Jesus, Christianity accepts that there can be such a thing as a 'just war'. A just war should satisfy these 5 conditions:

PROPER AUTHORITY A war must be declared by a proper authority, e.g. an elected government, a president or a monarch.

JUST CAUSE A war must have a just cause, e.g. self-defence, or reclaiming lost territory.

JUST AIM A war must have a just aim, and should stop when that aim has been achieved.

DISCRIMINATION A war must be waged without endangering civilians (i.e. with discrimination).

PROPORTIONALITY A war must be waged without undue force (i.e. with proportionality) — don't use a nuclear missile against someone with a bow and arrow.

A 'Holy War' is one where people believe God is 'on their side' — e.g. in the 11th, 12th and 13th centuries, Christians went on crusades to 'free' the holy places in Palestine.

"Declare a Holy War. Call the troops to arms."
Joel 3:9

Pacifists and Martyrs

1) A pacifist is someone who has strongly-held beliefs that war and physical violence are wrong under any circumstances.
2) There were pacifists in Britain who refused to fight in the world wars. These 'conscientious objectors' went to prison — they were prisoners of conscience.
3) They suffered humiliation in prison and after they'd been released.
4) Martyrs are prepared to die for their faith. This willingness to sacrifice your own life for what you believe in is fundamental to Christianity (see page 45) and other religions.
5) Many people risk their lives today by preaching the Gospel of Jesus and speaking out against governments (see page 28).

The Quakers are a Christian denomination opposed to war under all circumstances.

"Put your sword back in its place. All who draw the sword will die by the sword."
Matthew 26:52

Unconventional War — Nuclear War and Terrorism

Terrorism and nuclear war could both be described as unconventional warfare.

1) Terrorism is a form of violent protest that goes on all over the world.
2) Terrorists target any person, building or institution that could help their cause.
3) All Christian denominations are against nuclear weapons and weapons of mass destruction, because these weapons don't discriminate between civilians and people fighting the war.
4) The Church of England wants countries to reduce the number of nuclear weapons they have. However, it recognises that unilateral disarmament (where just one country gives up its weapons) is a difficult thing for a government to do.
5) That's why it calls for countries to work together and agree on multilateral disarmament, where many countries give up their arms at the same time.

Just war, just cause, just aim — just learn it pal...

People go to war for all kinds of reason, and there's nearly always a war or some kind of terrorist activity going on somewhere in the world. For the Exam, it's worth learning about a current conflict, especially why it started, and what efforts are being made to end it. Then you can include something topical in your answers.

Judaism & Islam

Judaism, Islam and War

Despite the fact that there have been a number of wars between Muslims and Jews, there are many similarities in the way the two religions approach the subject of war.

The Jewish View — Obligatory and Optional Wars

1) The universal greeting amongst Jews is 'shalom' (peace) — this is the ideal. War is hated, but there's a belief that war is sometimes necessary to bring about peace.
2) War is divided into two categories — milchemet mitzvah (obligatory war) and milchemet reshut (optional war).
3) An obligatory war might be:
   - i) a war fought in self-defence.
   - ii) a pre-emptive strike in order to avoid being attacked — the Six-Day War in 1967 for example.
   - iii) a war to help neighbouring countries — so that your own country is not invaded.
   - iv) a war commanded by God.
4) An optional war should only take place when all attempts to secure peace have failed.
5) No war should be fought to colonise or take revenge. This is forbidden.

The Six-Day War

In June 1967, Israel launched a series of attacks against its much larger Arab neighbours, destroying the Egyptian Air Force on the ground. After six days' fighting, Israel had won a war against Egypt, Jordan and Syria.

The Islamic View — 'Hate Your Enemy Mildly'

Muslims believe that war is sometimes necessary, although the concept of jihad is often misunderstood. These passages sum up Muslim teaching:

"The person who struggles so that Allah's word is supreme is the one serving Allah's cause." Hadith

"Hate your enemy mildly; he may be your friend one day." Hadith

Jihad — there are Two Kinds

1) There are two kinds of jihad (or 'striving')...

i) a Greater Jihad, which is when a Muslim makes a special effort to be a 'pure' Muslim, or fights against his or her own selfish desires.

ii) a Lesser Jihad — war is an example of a lesser jihad, but it must be fought only as a last resort. These wars are often thought of as 'Holy Wars'.

See page 93 for more about jihad.

2) Military jihad has very strict rules, and is similar to the Christian idea of a 'just war':
   - i) It is justified if it will bring about freedom from tyranny, restore peace, combat oppression, or right injustice.
   - ii) It must not be used to colonise, suppress or impose Islam on non-believers.
   - iii) The sick, the elderly, women and children should not be harmed, the natural world must not be damaged, and indiscriminate killing should be avoided.
   - iv) Jihad must be in the name of Allah, and according to his will. It must be declared by a religious leader, not any old politician.
   - v) Dying in the service of Allah turns a Muslim into a martyr. True martyrs go straight to paradise as an instant reward — martyrs don't have to wait for the Day of Judgement.
3) There is no real concept of pacifism in Islam, although peace is always the goal of war.

Peace, love and harmony — seems that's what we all want...

Judaism and Islam seem to have quite a lot in common when you find out a bit more about them. That's true when it comes to war and peace as well. Neither religion believes in unwavering pacifism — the attitude of both religions is that war is sometimes necessary, though always (and inevitably) unpleasant.

Religion and Drugs

Christianity, Judaism, Islam & general

Everyone has a view on drugs and drug abuse. But not all drugs are the same — and there are 3 kinds you especially need to know about:

HARD Drugs like heroin and cocaine — these are Class A drugs, the most serious category.

SOFT Although soft drugs are still illegal in Britain (Class B or C), they're not regarded as being so bad, and penalties for possessing these aren't as harsh as for hard drugs. Cannabis is widely seen as a soft drug. Drugs like ecstasy and amphetamines (speed) are often put in this category too.

SOCIAL Social drugs include alcohol and tobacco. Cannabis is viewed by some people as a social drug.

Christianity, Judaism and Islam all say Drugs are Bad

"Your body is a temple of the Holy Spirit..." — Although this is a line from the New Testament (1 Corinthians 6:19), the message is similar for Islam, Christianity and Judaism. Drugs are seen as bad, as they damage the mind, abuse the body God has given to us, and can lead to poverty or even death.

1) Illegal drugs are completely disapproved of by Christianity, Judaism and Islam — they're seen as a way of escaping the realities of life, and existing instead in an artificial fantasy world.

2) All three religions teach that the mind and the body are gifts from God, and that we do not have the right to abuse them. On a more practical level, drug taking is also seen as leading to irresponsible behaviour (e.g. neglecting your family or responsibilities), and possibly criminal activity.
3) Drugs taken to enhance performance in sport are also disapproved of, as they do not allow a person to properly display the skills they have been given. Again, they create a false world.

CANNABIS — THE SUBJECT OF MUCH RECENT DEBATE

Cannabis has been hotly debated recently. Some people believe it may have medical benefits, although others say it's a 'gateway drug', meaning users are more likely to end up using harder drugs. Although cannabis is now a Class C drug, it's still illegal — but many people (including some doctors, policemen and politicians) would like to see it legalised. Some say that drugs like ecstasy should also be legalised.

Islam is against cannabis for the same reasons it's against alcohol. And Sheik Ibn Tayumiyyah (a famous scholar and Islamic teacher) had this to say on the subject: "Sinful people smoke hashish (i.e. cannabis)... it disturbs the mind and temperament... excites sexual desire."

The Religions have Different Views on Alcohol

1) Christianity allows the consumption of alcohol — it's used in Holy Communion after all. However, drunkenness is frowned upon. Some denominations (e.g. The Salvation Army) are more disapproving than others.
2) Likewise in Judaism, alcohol is permitted, although drinking to excess is disapproved of. The Midrash (a collection of moral stories) contains the line, *"wine enters, sense goes out."*
3) Alcohol is forbidden in Islam, as it causes people to lose control — it's seen as a weapon of Shaytan (the Devil). A Muslim should have a clear mind when praying, and so there can be no place for alcohol.
4) Tobacco isn't mentioned in the Torah or the Qur'an — not surprising, as it hadn't been discovered when they were written. However, it's harmful to the body, and so should really be avoided.

See also page 93.

So I take it Jimi Hendrix wasn't a Muslim then...

This is a social issue that's often in the news. And as it's a very 'people-oriented' issue, you'd expect all religions to have something to say on the matter. But it's a Perspectives topic, so come Exam time, you can mention your own opinions, as well as the latest stuff from the news, and so on. That's what makes this subject interesting — often there are no right or wrong answers necessarily, just different opinions.

General

Religion and the Media

The term 'media' refers to any form of mass communication. So it'd be stuff like television, radio, newspapers, magazines, film, the Internet... Blah-de-blah-de-blah...

The Media is Becoming More Important

1) The amount of money spent on the media has become massive in recent years — especially with the recent launch of satellite and digital television, and the Internet.
2) At the same time, church attendances have been falling dramatically.
3) So as the role of the media in our lives increases, the role of organised religion declines in importance.

There are Religious Programmes on the Telly

1) The majority of television programming is secular (non-religious), although there are a few dedicated religious programmes to be found, as well as religious content in drama and current affairs programmes.
2) Traditionally the BBC has always transmitted religious programmes on a Sunday — during the so-called 'God slot'. The programmes themselves are nearly always Christian.
3) The best-known religious show is probably 'Songs of Praise' — on the BBC at around six o'clock on Sunday. It's broadcast from different locations, and focuses on a particular religious community and their church each week. BBC Radio 4 also broadcasts religious programmes on a Sunday.
4) On a Sunday, you can usually find a service of morning worship on one of the terrestrial television channels. This is to allow those who can't get to church (or those who would prefer to worship in private) to take part in an act of worship.

5) Evangelical Christian preachers can also be seen on television in the USA, and increasingly on cable and satellite TV in the UK. They speak to people in their homes, deliver God's message and raise money.
6) There are no specifically Jewish programmes on television, and this is a cause of concern and frustration for the Jewish community. Many feel that Jewish issues are often not dealt with fairly, and Jews are portrayed in a stereotypical way.
7) At its best, the media can be used to educate people about a particular faith or issue. However, misrepresentation and bias are a serious concern for followers of all faiths. Muslims and Jews especially often feel that they are sidelined or misrepresented in TV news and other forms of media.

Some other religious (or part-religious) programmes:
1) 'The Heaven and Earth Show' — covers a variety of religious and secular issues from the point of view of various faiths.
2) 'Black Britain' — often deals with issues important to the Muslim community.
3) 'East' — another programme concentrating on issues of interest to Muslim, Hindu and Sikh communities in the UK.
4) 'Everyman' and 'Heart of the Matter' — religious documentary programmes.

I've told you before — The Simpsons is NOT a religion...

There's not an awful lot of religion on the TV or in the newspapers. And because of the nature of the media, when religion is covered, it's more likely to be a story about an extreme weirdy cult than about people practising their faiths quietly, as they have done for years. It's the nature of the job, I guess.

Religion and the Media

General

It's not just religious TV programmes that grapple with the important issues of the day, however. There's also Dale Winton, Graham Norton, the Teletubbies... and others I don't have room for in a short page intro.

Soaps and Newspapers tackle Difficult Issues

1) Soap operas also deal with moral and spiritual issues. In recent years euthanasia, HIV, homosexuality, prostitution, celibacy, lesbianism, incest, death, marriage, infidelity and racism have all been covered in soaps (although rarely all in the same episode).
2) Even though soaps are often seen as a form of escapism, they enable us to see how a variety of characters deal with issues and emotions that we all may face at some point in our lives.
3) However, characters are sometimes criticised for being one-dimensional stereotypes. The same might also be said of characters in comedy programmes — they can easily cause offence to people.

1) Newspapers carry a range of stories, e.g. coverage of wars, terrorism, racist crime and refugees, as well as a variety of moral issues. This is where many people find out the 'truth'.
2) But some people worry about how the ideas of the people who own or write for newspapers affect their content. This might include political bias or a degree of xenophobia (i.e. hatred of foreigners). You might find completely different versions of the same story in 'The Daily Telegraph', 'The Sun', 'The Guardian' and 'The Daily Mail'.

The Media can also be a Bad Influence

1) Many people worry about the way the media influences people, especially children. Their main concerns are about how scenes containing sex, violence, bad language and drug taking might affect the young.
2) In the UK there's a 'watershed' — for the BBC this is 9pm. After this time, programmes are aimed at adults, and it's the responsibility of parents to decide whether children watch or not. However, before this time "*...all programmes...should be suitable for a general audience, including children.*"
3) There are also strict guidelines on sex, bad language and the treatment of religious issues.
4) However, some people would argue that sex, violence and other unsuitable material has been creeping into mainstream programming, and that this reflects a general lack of morals in society.
5) Sometimes the content of television programmes, films, newspapers and books is considered blasphemous, meaning that it's caused offence to followers of a specific faith. Salman Rushdie's novel 'The Satanic Verses' caused great offence to Muslims around the world.

Reflection or Cause...

Some people say that violence on TV reflects what already happens in society. But others say that it has a direct influence on society, and makes violence more likely. The same argument is used in relation to drugs, sexual behaviour, and so on.

Some Issues are Specific to Certain Types of Media

1) Films are officially classified to warn people about their content, and they may be censored too (i.e. the makers might be told to cut certain bits out). Some films urge 'parental guidance' (PG), while others are only deemed suitable for people over a certain age (e.g. 15 or 18).
2) More recently there have been grave concerns about the Internet, and the ease with which it can be used to access various materials — pornography, for example.
3) Advertisements have also been criticised for using sexual images to sell products to children.

Eastenders — real life stuff or total pap? Cast your votes...

People sometimes say that programmes on TV chip away at the moral fabric of society. What shocks us today will seem normal tomorrow. But those in the TV industry usually dispute that they have any kind of detrimental effect on society. Yep, once again, there's no right or wrong answer... just points of view.

Revision Summary

I bet you thought Religious Studies was all about God and churches and stuff. Little did you know that you'd be learning about environmental issues, war, terrorism, crime, punishment and the rest. But RS is all about things that affect people. So lucky, lucky you... you get to learn about all this malarky. But just to check that you've learnt all you need to know, have a go at these questions. You'll probably get them all right (well, you might, anyway). But if you get any wrong, go back and check out the relevant bit of the section, and then have another go at the questions. If you can get all the answers right, you'll be making life that much easier for yourself come Exam time.

1) What did the Brandt Report say about poverty?
2) What does the Bible say about how Christians should treat the poor?
3) How does the work of 'Christian Aid' reflect Christian teaching on poverty?
4) Describe Jewish thinking behind the idea of tzedaka.
5) What is meant by 'gemilut hasadim'?
6) What does zakah mean in Islam? And sadaqah?
7) What kinds of occupations would be seen as immoral in: a) Christianity? and, b) Islam?
8) Name 2 of the major environmental problems facing the earth.
9) What do Christians mean by 'stewardship' when discussing the environment?
10) Name a Christian organisation that works to help look after the environment.
11) Describe Jewish teaching on environmental issues.
12) Why do Muslims believe we should treat the world with love and respect?
13) Describe Christian teaching on the use of animals by humankind.
14) What are the views of Judaism on: a) eating meat? and b) animal experimentation?
15) Describe what a Muslims means by 'khalifah', when talking about the world we live in.
16) Describe the difference between a sin and a crime.
17) Give 6 reasons why someone might think it's right to punish someone who breaks the law.
18) Describe some non-religious views people may have about capital punishment.
19) What 5 conditions must a war satisfy for Christianity to regard it as 'just'?
20) Why are all Christian denominations against nuclear weapons?
21) Explain the following words: a) martyr, b) pacifist.
22) What is the difference between milchemet mitzvah and milchemet reshut?
23) Explain the difference between a greater jihad and a lesser jihad.
24) Explain why nuclear conflict could not be regarded as 'jihad' by a Muslim.
25) Explain why a) Christianity, b) Judaism, and c) Islam are opposed to drug-taking.
26) What is the attitude of Christianity and Judaism to the use of alcohol?
    Why is alcohol forbidden in Islam?
27) Why is there no mention of smoking in the Bible or the Qur'an?
28) Why might some religious believers feel that they are misrepresented or unfairly portrayed by the media?
29) Explain what is meant by television being a) a reflection of society, and b) a bad influence on society.
30) What is meant by the term 'watershed'? And 'censorship'?
31) Why is the Internet a particular cause of concern when trying to prevent children viewing pornography?

Basic Christian Beliefs

Worship offered to Jesus is what distinguishes Christianity from all other monotheistic (one-god) religions. While not all Christians believe exactly the same things, most accept the doctrines of the Apostles' Creed.

The Apostles' Creed — a Summary of the Christian Faith

The Apostles' Creed summarises the basic Christian teachings about Jesus: *'Creed' just means a set of beliefs.*

① **Jesus is the Christ** 'Christ' isn't a surname — it means the same as 'Messiah', i.e. 'Anointed One of God'.

② **The Incarnation** This was the act by which God became a human being. Note that Christians don't believe Jesus was 'half God and half man' — he was fully both.

③ **The Virgin Birth** The Gospels say that Jesus was born of a virgin — Mary became pregnant through the influence of the Holy Spirit. This is why Christians say "God's Son", or "God the Son".

④ **The Crucifixion** It was Jesus' death on the cross which won his people forgiveness of sin.

⑤ **The Resurrection** Jesus rose from the dead on Easter Day, and is still alive today.

⑥ **The Ascension** After the resurrection Jesus 'ascended into Heaven' (not necessarily 'in the sky').

1) The Apostles' Creed also includes important teaching about the Holy Spirit.
2) Although Christians believe in only one God, this God exists in 3 forms — God the Father, God the Son and God the Holy Spirit. Together, these three make up the Trinity.
3) The Holy Spirit is God's influence in the world, and is often pictured as fire, or as a dove, or thought of as wind.

After the Ascension, God sent his Spirit down upon Jesus' followers in 'tongues of fire' at Pentecost (see page 61).

At Jesus' baptism the Spirit descended on him in the form of a dove.

There's some more basic Christian beliefs on pages 6 and 8.

Jesus sets an Example for Christians today

Jesus' Example of Self-sacrifice and Suffering

Christians believe that in his willingness to suffer and die on their behalf, Jesus set an example which they themselves should be prepared to follow. In Mark 8:34 Jesus says, "*If anyone would come after me... he must deny self and take up his cross and follow me.*"

Jesus' Death

1) Christians believe that Jesus' death was not a sign of his failure, but the climax of his ministry.
2) In dying on the cross, Jesus paid for all the sin of mankind. Because he himself was sinless, and because he was God Incarnate as well as Man, his death was able to redeem mankind.
3) The Bible teaches that God is merciful, but he is also just, so our sins have to be paid for. Jesus sacrificed himself in order to pay that price.

Jesus' Resurrection

1) In rising from death, Jesus demonstrated to Christians the truth of his claims, and proved that the debt of man's sin had been paid. He also demonstrated that there is life after death.
2) Christians believe that everyone who has died will be 'resurrected' at the Last Judgement (this is a personal day of judgement, not the same one for everybody). Those that God finds acceptable as a result of Jesus' sacrifice will enter Heaven — the rest will not.

Three into one doesn't go in maths — but this is RS...

Remember, that stuff about the Trinity doesn't mean that Christians believe in three Gods — they're just different forms of the same God. It's a bit like the way water can be steam, ice or, well, water — it's all the same thing really, just in different forms. Reminds me of those transformer toys you used to get... sort of.

The Bible

The Bible is a collection of books in different styles and languages written over a period of about 1000 years. It's also the Christian Scriptures — meaning that for Christians, it's sacred.

The Bible — the Old and New Testaments

The Bible's divided into 2 main parts — the Old and New Testaments:

THE OLD TESTAMENT

The Old Testament is the Jewish Scriptures (i.e. it's considered sacred by Jews). Written in Hebrew and Aramaic, its 39 books include the Creation story, the books of the Law (Torah), the 10 Commandments, various histories of Ancient Israel, prophecy, poetry and psalms.

THE NEW TESTAMENT

The New Testament is the specifically Christian part of the Bible. Written in Greek in the 1st Century CE, its 27 books include the 4 Gospels, the Acts of the Apostles (describing the early years of Christianity), 13 letters by St Paul (giving advice about the Christian life), 8 letters by other early Christian leaders, and the Revelation of St John — an apocalyptic vision.

The 4 Gospels are Matthew, Mark, Luke (called the Synoptic Gospels, as they are all very similar stories of Jesus), and John (which portrays Jesus in a very different way).
The word 'Gospel' means 'good news', and the Gospels tell the good news about Jesus Christ.

The Bible is used as a Christian Faith Guidebook

Christians accept the Bible as authoritative in forming their beliefs and guiding their actions.

1) Christians believe the Bible offers directions for living a moral life. It presents Jesus Christ as our example for godly living, and teaches that we best love God by showing love to others.
2) Both the Old and New Testaments (but especially the New) include rituals for worship, large parts of which are still included in modern worship services (e.g. Holy Communion and baptism).
3) The faith of the Roman Catholic Church is based largely on the Scriptures, but Catholic tradition and the Magisterium (i.e. the teaching of the pope, his cardinals and bishops) are also very important.
   The Protestant Churches claim their authority mainly from the Scriptures.
4) Different groups of Christians interpret the Bible in different ways (according to their own conscience):

① **Literalism** Many Christians believe that pretty well everything in the Bible is literally true, e.g. Jesus really did 'walk on water'.

Some people argue that there are contradictions in the Bible, and so it's impossible for everything to be literally true.

② **Fundamentalism** This is a form of literalism. Fundamentalists believe that it's wrong to question anything in the Bible, since it was dictated by God.

③ **Conservative View** This view is probably the most common among Christians. They believe that the Bible was inspired by God but not dictated — the writers' own interests also come through. Readers must use their intelligence and the guidance of the Holy Spirit in order to understand the writers' intentions.

④ **Liberal View** Liberals believe that pretty well everything in the Bible can be interpreted 'symbolically', e.g. Jesus didn't really 'walk on water' — the story has some other 'spiritual' meaning.

The Bible has been Influential for Centuries

1) There are many different versions of the Bible in use today, and loads of translations into other languages.
2) The Gospels (which contain the teachings of Jesus) are central to Christian faith.
3) Christians often meet to study the Bible and to pray, and it's also read for guidance, or as an act of devotion towards God.

The Bible — sells more than any revision guide...

The Bible has profoundly affected countless lives (e.g. the saints, missionaries, campaigners for social change), and arguments over its interpretation continue to be a legal matter in some countries — e.g. courts in the USA have had to legislate recently on whether schools should teach the Bible's Creation story as fact or fable.

Christian Values

Christians, like all people with a religious faith, try to act in a way consistent with their beliefs.

The Ten Commandments — show some Respect

Jesus was a Jew, so his values were grounded in Jewish belief. There are 613 commandments in the Torah (see page 74), but the most famous are the Decalogue (i.e. the Ten Commandments) — found in Exodus 20:

1) You shall have no other Gods before me.
2) You shall not bow down before idols.
3) You shall not misuse the name of the Lord.
4) Observe the Sabbath and keep it holy.
5) Honour your father and mother.
6) You shall not murder.
7) You shall not commit adultery.
8) You shall not steal.
9) You shall not give false testimony (lie).
10) You shall not covet (want someone else's stuff).

Basically the 10 Commandments are about showing respect — to God, and to other people.

Jesus said, "Don't just Respect — Love"

1) Jesus' Jewish opponents often accused him of breaking religious laws — he healed people on the Sabbath when Jews were not supposed to do any work, for example.

   But Jesus said he wasn't trying to undermine the law — "Do not think I have come to do away with the Law of Moses... I have come to fulfil it." Matthew 5:17.

2) Jesus thought the Jewish authorities had missed the point of God's Law, and that the 'spirit' of the law was more important than the 'letter'. He believed that if you were a good person, you'd do good things.
3) In fact, he taught that your motivation was even more important than your actions — being angry with someone could be just as bad as killing them (Matthew 5:21-22).
4) For Jesus, even respect wasn't enough — he wanted his followers to love. When asked which was the most important commandment, he gave a pretty neat answer which summed up his beliefs...

   "The most important one is this... love the Lord your God with all your heart, soul, mind and strength; the second is this: love your neighbour as you love yourself." — Mark 12:28-31

Four Types of Love — Eros, Philia, Storge and Agape

At the Last Judgement (Matthew 25:31-46), Jesus says that we shall all be judged according to whether or not we helped those in need. This is a form of love, but it has little to do with 'liking' and everything to do with serving. Ancient Greek actually had four words for 'love':

1. EROS — this is erotic or sexual love, based on physical attraction.
2. PHILIA — this is friendship. It involves 'give and take', and is usually between equals.
3. STORGE — or affection, as felt between members of a family, or as affection for pets, places, and so on.
4. AGAPE — this is Christian love, a reflection of the love God has for us. It gives without needing to take.

In the Parable of The Good Samaritan (Luke 10:25-37), the Samaritan demonstrates love (agape) by giving practical help to a 'neighbour' in trouble. See page 26 for more info.

In some versions of the Bible, 'agape' is translated as 'charity'.

Agape is a Guiding Christian Principle

...the Bible says so.

1 John 4:7-21 encourages Christians to love because love comes from God, and that someone who doesn't love doesn't know God. God showed his love for us by sending his son so that our sins could be forgiven.

1 Corinthians 13 is a famous passage summarising the Apostle Paul's concept of love. He says that it matters more than faith or hope, or anything.

"Love is patient and kind. It envies no one, is never boastful... rude... selfish, or quick to take offence. Love keeps no score of wrongs... There is nothing love cannot face... love never ends."

And see page above for more about Mark 12:28-31.

Love never ends — I am the walrus, goo, goo, ga joob...

Respect and love are the basic principles of Christianity — but that doesn't mean that they can provide easy answers to complex questions. However, they give you a place to start thinking, which can sometimes help.

Love and Forgiveness

Love is all around us — it's everywhere I go. That's good news. But Jesus said forgiveness is also important.

Love and Forgiveness go Together

1) Christianity teaches that forgiveness comes from love, and that love needs forgiveness.
2) Jesus taught that God is always ready to forgive us, but we must accept that forgiveness, and forgive others in turn.
3) Forgiveness is also closely related to repentance. Christians believe that God's forgiveness can only be activated in our lives when we repent of our sins (i.e. say we are sorry, and turn our backs on them).
4) If we repent, and put our faith in God, God forgives us and we are reconciled with him. Christians believe the same sort of reconciliation is needed between people.

Zacchaeus the tax collector (Luke 19:1-10)
A story illustrating Jesus putting forgiveness into practice... Jesus goes as a guest to the home of the hated tax collector Zacchaeus, whose life is completely changed after he decides to repent.

Forgiveness and Punishment

1) Jesus taught that people should not seek revenge when wronged — they should 'turn the other cheek'. But this doesn't mean being a submissive victim — just that we should base our response on the principles of love and forgiveness.
2) For example, most Christians don't believe that if someone commits a crime, we should do nothing. They believe punishment can be more constructive. Punishment can be used to reform an offender and to deter others from offending, as well as for retribution.
3) Likewise with bullying — it may be right to face up to the situation and sort it out, rather than allow someone to become a victim. But once the situation has been sorted, Christians believe we must 'forgive and forget', and not remain bitter.

Dick's 'turn the other cheek' philosophy seemed somehow inappropriate, given the circumstances.

It Sounds Easy — but it can get very Complicated...

Jesus' teachings aren't simplistic, however. And they're certainly not a recipe for a life full of easy decisions. E.g. if a woman wants an abortion, should we be trying to show love to *her*, or to the *foetus*... And can we base moral decisions about things like contraception, genetic engineering, and global warming on love alone...

In practice, Christians seek to base their moral decisions on:

1) Love
2) Scripture — for guidance,
3) Conscience — their own sense of right and wrong,
4) Advice — from people they respect,
5) Tradition — authority of Church tradition.

Tricky Questions — The Criminal Justice System and the Welfare State

Christian values can be applied to all kinds of real-life situations...

1) It can be hard to decide which matters more — compassion or justice. For example, in dealing with criminals, is it more 'loving' to let them off, or to punish them... Not an easy question to answer.
2) Similarly, in seeking to help the underprivileged, does giving too much help create dependency... (i.e. do they become too reliant on that help).
3) Christians helped create the Welfare State in Britain after World War 2. In a welfare state the government protects citizens' economic wellbeing, providing free health care, education, and so on.
4) But does this lead people to take things for granted, and not strive to improve their own lives... Margaret Thatcher thought so. She believed it was better to create an enterprise culture — she wanted people to take more responsibility for themselves, and the state to do less. But is this fair to everyone...

So that's where Wet Wet Wet got those lyrics...

By preaching 'love your enemies', Christianity isn't trying to tell everyone that they need to be a submissive victim. But it does mean exercising a bit of imagination when it comes to responding to difficult situations.

The Sermon on the Mount

Some say the Sermon on the Mount preaches an ideal which no one can live up to. But others argue that Christians can still aspire to this ideal, though no one can be totally perfect (this side of the grave, anyway).

The Sermon on the Mount — the Christian Ideal

The Sermon on the Mount is one of the most important summaries of Jesus' moral teaching found in the Gospels. It appears as a collection in Matthew 5:1 - 7:29, but much of the same material is also in Luke.

The Beatitudes (Matthew 5:3-12) and the Teaching on 'Salt and Light' (Matthew 5:13-16)

The sermon begins with a passage on true happiness (what it means to be 'blessed') — this is not to be found in wealth or pride, but in a simple, humble life lived in obedience to God.

"Blessed are the meek, for they will inherit the earth."

Jesus' followers are meant to be 'salt and light', i.e. a source of godly influence in the world.

"You are the salt of the earth."

Jesus' Reinterpretation of the Law of Moses (Matthew 5:17-48)

See page 47.

Jesus speaks about anger, adultery, divorce, vows, revenge and love for our enemies.

"If someone strikes you on the right cheek, turn to him the other also."

'Displaying Religion' (Matthew 6:1-18)

Good deeds must not be done for show, but for God.
Prayer must be sincere. (The Lord's Prayer is in this bit as well.)

"Our Father in heaven, hallowed be your name..."

Christians and Money (Matthew 6:19-34)

"You cannot serve God and Money." Also Earthly riches are useless, but spiritual riches last for ever.

Christians and Judgement (Matthew 7:1-5)

Christians should not pass judgement on others — that's God's job. It's also hypocrisy.

"Why do you look at the speck of sawdust in your brother's eye and pay no attention to the plank in your own eye?"

The Golden Rule (Matthew 7:7-12)

"Do to others what you would have them do to you, for this sums up the Law and the Prophets."

Christian Values in Action

Christians have found various ways of expressing these values in action. Christian vocations include:

- **Service to others** (in health work, education etc.)
- **Showing compassion to those who suffer** (e.g. visiting hospices for the dying)
- **Seeking justice for the oppressed** (e.g. seeking to help political prisoners)

People seek to be 'Salt and Light' in Different Ways

Loads of people have tried to be 'salt and light' in their own individual ways. Here are two obvious examples:

Dr Martin Luther King

A Baptist minister who dedicated his life to trying to change the way black people were treated in the USA — they earned only half as much as whites, and many were not allowed to vote, or go to 'white only' public places.

Despite death threats he organised many types of peaceful protest — marches, rallies, boycotts and so on. In 1965 blacks were given equal voting rights with whites, but in 1968 King was assassinated aged only 39.

Mother Teresa

She was an Albanian Roman Catholic nun who devoted herself to the destitute and dying in Calcutta, India. She founded the Order of the Missionaries of Charity, whose nuns now work amongst the poor all over the world. She said that it isn't what you do for God that counts, but how much love you pour into it. She won the Nobel Peace Prize in 1979, and died in 1997 at the age of 87.

Don't pass judgement on others — that's the examiner's job...

Most Christians believe that they should seek to discover what God is calling them to do. There are some examples above, but there are millions of others. And when it comes to writing about individual Christians who've tried to be 'salt and light', it's probably best to choose people that you have an interest in.

Spreading the Gospel

Christians believe it's wrong to display their religion just for show (see page 49). However, most Christians do think it's important for them to stand up for their beliefs, and not be a 'secret Christian'.

The Great Commission — 'Spread the Gospel'

1) Jesus told his followers to 'spread the gospel' (Matthew 28:19-20), so that other people would have the chance to become Christians too.
2) He also taught that they were to be 'salt and light' in society (see page 49).

Christians therefore seek to challenge society around them in 2 ways...

> 1) They seek to challenge people's beliefs.
> 2) They seek to challenge people's behaviour.

'Mature' Christians seek to present this challenge by means of their own words and conduct. They see that it's very important for their actions to mirror their words — otherwise they would just be hypocrites. (Of course this doesn't mean that, in practice, no Christian is a hypocrite.)

Challenging Beliefs — easy does it...

1) Many Christians like the chance to talk about their faith with their family, friends and neighbours (and many feel it is their duty — see page 51). Some will even look for opportunities to do this in a wider context — e.g. they may write books or appear on TV.
2) Putting forward reasoned arguments to support your religious beliefs is called apologetics.
3) Evangelical Christians in particular consider it a priority to 'win people for Christ'. This is because they believe that a person can't get to Heaven unless they 'come to know Christ'.
4) However, people don't always appreciate their concern... No one likes to have religion 'rammed down their throat'. It's important to maintain a balance between saying too much and saying too little.

Challenging Behaviour — Absolute and Relative Morality

Christians don't always agree about how (if at all) they should try to influence the conduct of society.

1) Some Christians consider it wrong to 'impose their morals on other people' — while others think it's wrong to sit by and 'watch society go down the drain'.
2) This is why some Christians campaign vigorously against abortion, euthanasia, and so on — while others would prefer to let people make up their own minds. They believe it's more effective to show compassion than to act like a moral police force.
3) Also, some Christians strongly support the idea of absolute morality, which means that they think many things are always right or always wrong.
4) Others favour relative morality, which holds that most things are sometimes right and sometimes wrong, depending on the circumstances. This view is sometimes called situation ethics.

Jesus' own attitude is summed up in John 8:1-11, where a woman who has committed adultery is to be stoned by a crowd.

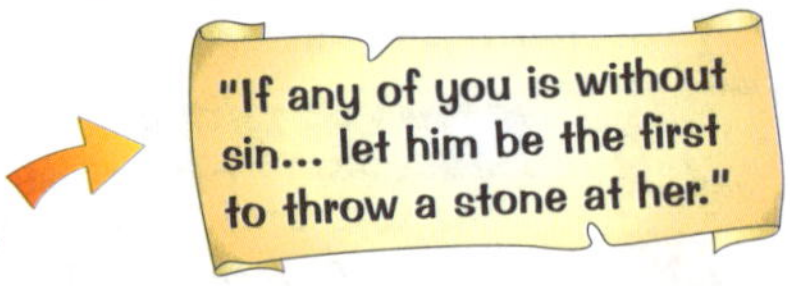

I never preach — except to tell you to learn this stuff...

Christian ethics have influenced society in a powerful way over the years. For example, Christians in Britain and elsewhere have been very much involved in the abolition of slavery, the provision of education for all, legislation against child labour, and more. Most people today would consider that this has been a good thing. However, Christian attempts to limit the availability of abortion, the amount of violence shown on TV or the rights of homosexuals have proved much more controversial.

Living the Christian Life

All practising Christians seek to obey the instructions of the Great Commission (see page 50), but they do this in different ways, depending on their denomination, culture, background, personal taste or talents.

'Witnessing for Christ' — the Duty of Every Christian

1) Evangelicals (who can belong to any denomination or to a specifically evangelical church) particularly stress the importance of conversion. Others put more emphasis on praying for the souls of unbelievers.
2) But all true Christians acknowledge the need to 'witness for Christ' in their speech and lives, so that those people they come into contact with may be given the opportunity to respond to Jesus.

THROUGH SPEECH

1) Christians often welcome opportunities to talk to non-Christians about their beliefs.
2) Churches of all denominations have in recent years been running 'Alpha Courses', which are designed to explain Christianity to those as yet outside the faith.
3) But many Christians find this sort of evangelism difficult, as non-Christians aren't always keen to listen.

THROUGH LIFESTYLE

1) Christians should try to live their lives based on love for God and for their neighbours (see page 47).
2) Jesus said, "*If you have love for one another, everyone will know you are my disciples.*" — John 13:35
3) Christians also seek to live by the Bible's moral code, with integrity, witnessing to Christ through their marriages, family life, work, how they spend their free time, and so on.

THROUGH VOCATION

1) Some Christians feel that God is calling them to full-time Christian work.
2) This may be as a deacon, priest or bishop, through charity or missionary work, or in a Christian community, e.g. as a monk or nun in a religious order.

Monks and Nuns are Members of Religious Orders

1) Those who adopt the monastic life of renunciation take vows of:
   i) *POVERTY*: a monk or nun must not be tied down by possessions, but 'hold everything in common'.
   ii) *CHASTITY*: a monk or nun may have no sexual relationships. They must seek intimacy with God.
   iii) *OBEDIENCE*: a monk or nun must be completely dedicated to God and to his/her community.
2) Some religious orders stress service to the poor/sick/destitute (called apostolic congregations). Others go in for prayer and study — usually involving 'enclosure', where members rarely if ever leave their monasteries (contemplative congregations).
3) Most Christians would agree that both are important aspects of Christian life, but that every Christian must find the right balance for him or herself.

'The Carmelites' and 'Poor Clares' (for women), and the 'Carthusians' or 'Cistercians' (for men) are examples of contemplative congregations.

Mother Teresa's 'Missionaries of Charity' (see page 49), and the 'Franciscans' are apostolic congregations.

L'Arche — A Religious Community at Work

1) L'Arche was founded in France by Roman Catholic Jean Vanier (who has been called a 'modern saint of the poor and servant of the handicapped').
2) He gave up his career as a teacher of philosophy in order to welcome disabled people into his home, so they wouldn't have to live in impersonal institutions.
3) His idea has inspired Christians of many denominations to do the same, and L'Arche houses now exist in several countries including the UK.

Religious orders — learn all this Christianity stuff well...

Depending on what syllabus you're studying, you might need to know about the purpose and practice of a religious community. L'Arche is just one example you could use, but don't feel as though it's the only one. Choose one that you're vaguely interested in, and study that.

The Church

The 'Church' traces its roots back to its founder, Jesus Christ. It's basically a community of believers. Those who profess faith in Jesus as God's promised Messiah become part of that community.

The Church — More than a Building

The mission of the Church is to teach that Jesus Christ is our Saviour, and to make people disciples for him. It does this by teaching the things Christ commanded, and also by teaching that his death on the cross is a means by which sins are forgiven, and that his resurrection confirms his identity as God's Messiah.

The Church as the Body of Christ

1) St Paul taught that the community of believers was the "Body of Christ" on Earth, with Christ as its head.
2) Christians who have died remain part of the faith community — this group is referred to as the Communion of Saints.
3) Christians believe the Church was called into existence by the Holy Spirit, and is therefore 'holy'.
4) Despite its fragmentation into various traditions and denominations, the Church claims a spiritual unity.
5) Ecumenism is work carried out by different churches aimed towards actual unity. This might include joint acts of worship or joint service in the community.

The Church has a Powerful Influence

The Pope has a massive influence over Roman Catholics — e.g. in respect of abortion and contraception (see p14).

1) The teachings of the Church on moral issues (such as abortion, sexuality, and social responsibility) continue to exert strong influence.
2) Church leaders are held in respect, and their pronouncements are adhered to by faithful followers.
3) The Church also offers guidance to those who believe they may be called by God into a specific vocation e.g. the ordained ministry, and the lay ministry (who aren't ordained, but who act for the Church in helping the needy).
4) The church also influences social and political development through its involvement in peace and justice movements.

The Church has Various Functions in the Community

The role and function of the local church is to put the Christian faith into action. It does this in the following ways:

i) by providing a regular pattern of worship,
ii) by providing 'rites of passage' — e.g. baptism, confirmation, weddings, funerals...
iii) by providing Christian teaching,
iv) by ministering to the sick and needy,
v) by supporting causes for justice and peace.

Church — place of worship, religious community, teenage singer...

Yep — don't go assuming that when the Exam asks a question about the Church, it's talking about that building near where you live that rings its bells once a week. It's a bit more than that. Anyway, as long as you know all of this stuff as well, then you should be okay on the 'Church' question in the Exam.

Traditions and Denominations

There are some significant variations among Christians' beliefs, which have sometimes led to heated conflict. But what they share is some kind of 'relationship with Christ'.

Three Main Traditions — Roman Catholic, Orthodox and Protestant

There have been a couple of major splits in the history of the Christian Church.

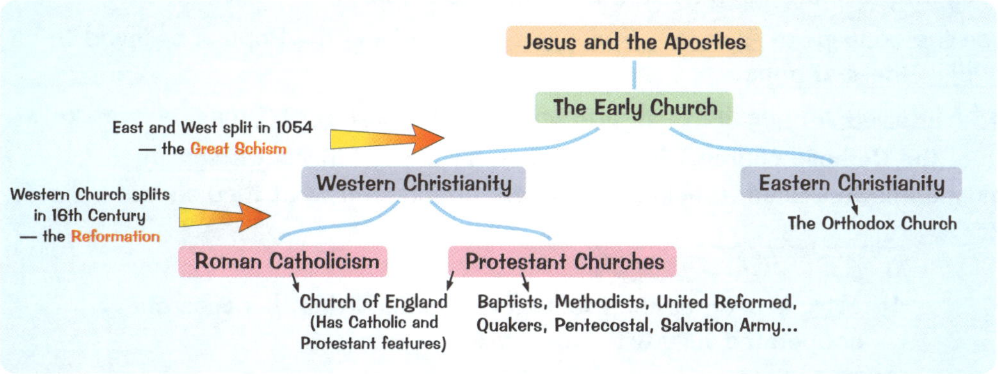

In the Great Schism, the Pope and the Orthodox Patriarch excommunicated each other from their churches.

The Reformation began when Martin Luther challenged the authority of the Pope.

Roman Catholics

1) Roman Catholics are all those Christians who accept the authority of the Bishop of Rome (the Pope).
2) They believe in the 7 Sacraments as 'vehicles of God's grace' (see page 62).
3) They respect the authority of the Bible, the traditions of the Church, and the Magisterium (see next page).

Protestants

1) Protestants base their beliefs and practices on the Reformation.
2) The Reformers stressed the importance of the Bible rather than Church Tradition or the teachings of the Pope.
3) Members of the Protestant clergy are usually referred to as ministers.

The Church of England has both Roman Catholic and Protestant features.

Orthodox Christians

1) Orthodox Christians are found mainly in Eastern Europe, Russia and what was the Greek-speaking part of the Roman Empire.
2) They believe that their clergy are in direct succession from the Apostles.
3) They also have 7 sacraments, and honour (but don't worship) icons — pictures of saints.

There are Loads of Protestant Denominations

The different groupings within Protestantism are known as denominations.
Numbers 2-7 below are known as the 'Nonconformists' or 'Free Churches'.

1) Anglicanism is the worldwide 'communion' of churches in fellowship with the parent Church of England. This is the 'established' (i.e. national) church in England. It's kind of between Catholicism and Protestantism — but there's a lot of variety within it. The 'more catholic' churches are known as Anglo-Catholic or 'high church'. Those that are more like Methodists are called 'low church'.
2) Methodists favour simple services where hymns and the sermon are particularly important.
3) Baptists believe in baptising only those who place their faith in Christ — rather than all babies.
4) Pentecostals favour the 'gifts of the Holy Spirit' — their worship includes plenty of enthusiastic singing.
5) Quakers are best known for their pacifism and for their largely silent services.
6) The Salvation Army is organised along military lines, and works particularly among the underprivileged.
7) The House Churches are informal groups that originally met in houses, but outgrew them.

Movers and Shakers — Cockney rhyming slang for Quakers... (maybe)

There are at least 20,800 denominations worldwide, so don't think that the above list is all there is to know. But at the same time, don't feel as though you need to know everything about all 20,800 — that would be a pretty tough assignment. Though not for God, obviously, because he's omniscient.

Traditions and Denominations

The Roman Catholic Church is the largest Christian group in the world.

The Roman Catholic Church has its own Customs

The Magisterium — this is the teaching authority of the Pope and bishops of the Roman Catholic Church. To Roman Catholics, the authority of the Church rivals that of the Bible itself.

1) The Magisterium rests on the concept of Apostolic Succession — meaning the Pope is believed to be a direct successor of St Peter, the first pope.
2) The Pope is believed to be infallible on questions of faith and morals (i.e. he can't make a mistake).
3) Dogmas are firm beliefs of the Catholic church. Most of them are set out in the Catechism — a series of questions and answers used to help its members understand what they should believe.

The Importance of Mary

1) Mary is seen as the model for Christian living, because she cooperated fully with God's will.
2) Catholic doctrine teaches that she was born without original sin, meaning she had none of the flaws that all other humans have — this is known as the Immaculate Conception.
3) She remained a virgin all her life, and after she died she was taken up to Heaven in the Assumption (see page 61).
4) Catholics don't worship Mary, but they do pray to her and ask her to pray for them (for example in the '*Ave Maria/Hail Mary*'). She is also known as 'Mother of God'.

Transubstantiation and the Mass

1) Virtually all Christians except the Salvation Army and the Quakers recognise the importance of Holy Communion (also called the Eucharist — or often 'Mass' by Roman Catholics), but most see it as just a symbol.
2) However, to Roman Catholics, by the power of the Holy Spirit, the bread and wine become the body and blood of Christ (this is known as transubstantiation), and it is through these that Jesus takes up residence in his people. This is why it's vital for Roman Catholics to attend Mass regularly.

See page 60 for more about Eucharist and the Mass.

Influential Movements in the 20th Century

Two movements profoundly affected 20th century Christianity across traditions and denominations:

1) The Charismatic Movement began in the Pentecostal churches, but later spread worldwide. It stresses the importance of 'spiritual gifts', such as speaking in tongues and prophecy. Charismatic Worship is characterised by expression of emotion (e.g. clapping or dancing), and is meant to be entirely spontaneous. There are charismatic groups among Roman Catholics and Anglicans, but most charismatics are evangelicals, who emphasise the importance of spreading the Gospel.
2) Liberation Theology began in Latin America with the aim of fighting oppression. It works by influencing national institutions (like those for health and education), but protest is also considered legitimate. Some priests even supported the use of violence as a last resort, since the regimes they fought against were causing entire populations to suffer.

There's something about Mary...

It's important to realise that not all Christians are the same. Roman Catholics make up the largest group of Christians, and so it's pretty important that you at least know something about them (and even more if you're doing one of the units dedicated to Roman Catholicism). Well, lots of stuff is important, I guess.

Members of the Church

This is a page full of bishops and priests and stuff.

The Roman Catholic Church has a Hierarchy...

The Roman Catholic Church is arranged in a hierarchy, with the Pope at the top.

THE POPE — The Bishop of Rome and head of the worldwide Roman Catholic Church. Jesus is believed to have chosen St Peter as the first pope, and the current pope is his spiritual descendent. On matters of faith and morals, the pope is regarded as infallible and binding upon all Roman Catholics (see also page 54).

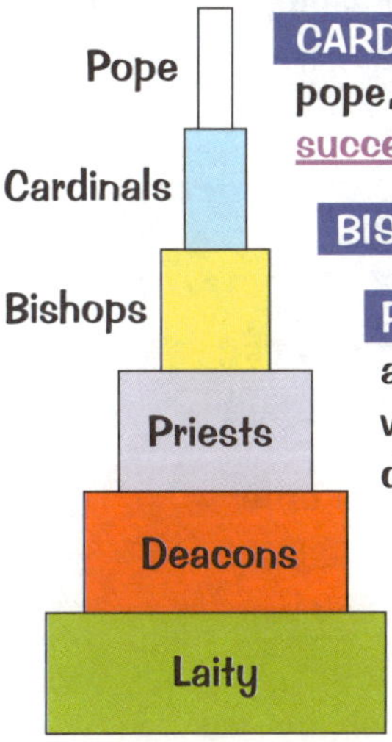

CARDINALS — The highest rank of bishop next to the pope. They're appointed by the pope, and act as his advisors. In turn, they're responsible for appointing the pope's successor. There's a cardinal for each country where there are Roman Catholics.

BISHOPS — Bishops are also appointed by the pope — one per diocese.

PRIESTS — The head of the local church in each Catholic parish, and answerable to the bishop. He's in overall charge of the Roman Catholic worship and education within that parish. Roman Catholic priests and deacons remain unmarried — they're 'married' to the Church.

DEACONS — A candidate for the priesthood is ordained as a deacon. He may preach and lead worship, but not celebrate holy communion.

These 3 offices are held by men who have been ordained, i.e. officially admitted into the priesthood by the Catholic Church.

LAITY — ordinary non-ordained Roman Catholics (or ordinary non-ordained Anglicans).

Holy Orders and Ordination

The act of ordination distinguishes members of the clergy from those who are laity. Ordination is conferred by the 'laying on of hands' by a bishop. Only priests and above can administer the sacraments of the Church. In the Roman Catholic Church, being ordained as a priest is called receiving the 'Sacrament of Holy Orders'.

Cathedral Staff

A cathedral is the central church of a diocese, and contains the throne of the bishop or archbishop. Cathedral life and worship is governed by a dean and a committee called a Chapter, who are assisted by the canons — priests appointed by the bishop onto the staff.

...and so do the Protestant and Orthodox Churches

1) The Anglican Church is also a hierarchy of bishops, priests and deacons, with the Archbishop of Canterbury (the head of the Church of England) at the top.
2) For much of its history women weren't allowed to be ordained, since Christ only ever commissioned men to administer the sacraments. This has now changed and there are women priests, but it remains a controversial issue. Anglican priests are allowed to marry.
3) In the Presbyterian Church, presbyters (or elders) are church leaders with the specific responsibility of preaching and teaching from the Bible. They're appointed by the local congregation and answerable to the church members when they meet.
4) In the Orthodox Church, patriarchs are at the head of each national church, with the Patriarch of Constantinople (or Istanbul) being the 'first among equals'. Men can become priests at 30, and are allowed to marry (but if they do, they can't become a bishop).

Lay ministers are non-ordained church members who are allowed to perform certain duties e.g. visiting the sick, leading worship.

It'd be a cardinal sin not to learn this page...

I bet you thought vicars would get a mention. Well, here you are. 'Vicar' is a general title that's come to be used to refer to any parish priest. 'Minister' is also a general title — used to describe anyone who's been ordained. And the clergy consists of anyone who's been ordained. Lots of words for the same kind of thing.

A Christian Church

A Christian place of worship is a church or chapel. Churches often have a similar layout to each other. (Chapels are usually smaller than churches, and not quite so fancy.)

The Location of a Church is often Symbolic

1) Christian churches are often found on tops of hills. This is because they would have been the most important building in the area, and so needed to be easy to see and defend.
2) Churches were traditionally built from local stone and materials which would have been easily available. The quality of the decoration and fittings reflected the church's status and wealth.
3) They were sometimes built on ancient pagan sites — sacred groves of trees, for example. Pagans were people who worshipped a number of different gods, a practice much more common before Christianity became popular.
4) The size of the church reflected the size and wealth of the parish, or the wealth and status of the local people.
5) Seen from above, churches were often built in the shape of a cross aligned from east to west, so that the church faces the rising sun. This is because east is the direction of the Holy Land where Jesus lived. It also symbolises God's goodness lighting up the darkness.

A Parish Church has some Typical Features

1) **TOWER** This draws people's eyes up to Heaven to remind people of God. It was also used in the past for defence, and houses the church bells.

2) **TRANSEPTS** The two wings of a cross-shaped church, at right angles to the nave (see page 57).

5) **WEATHER-VANE** This provided a medieval public service (weather was important to farmers), and is often in the shape of a cock to remind people of the story of St Peter.

(This is usually on top of the tower.)

3) **CHURCHYARD** This is consecrated ground surrounding the church, used for burials.

4) **GRAVESTONE** A stone memorial marking a grave.

6) **CHURCHYARD CROSS** The most important Christian symbol.

Many churches also have these extra features:

7) **PORCH** The day-to-day entrance.

8) **WEST DOOR** The main ceremonial entrance.

9) **LYCH-GATE** Coffins were placed in the gate to await the arrival of the minister to conduct the funeral service.

10) **NICHE** This is just a recess to hold a statue.

It's always crosses — why don't they build one in the shape of a fish?...

You find most parish churches built more than a century ago look pretty similar. Chapels tend to vary more, as do more modern chapels and churches. The Roman Catholic cathedral in Liverpool is very odd. Though kinda groovy... (if you like that kind of thing), but certainly not what you expect from a cathedral.

A Christian Church

Inside A Typical Parish Church

Roman Catholic and Church of England churches are often very similar in layout:

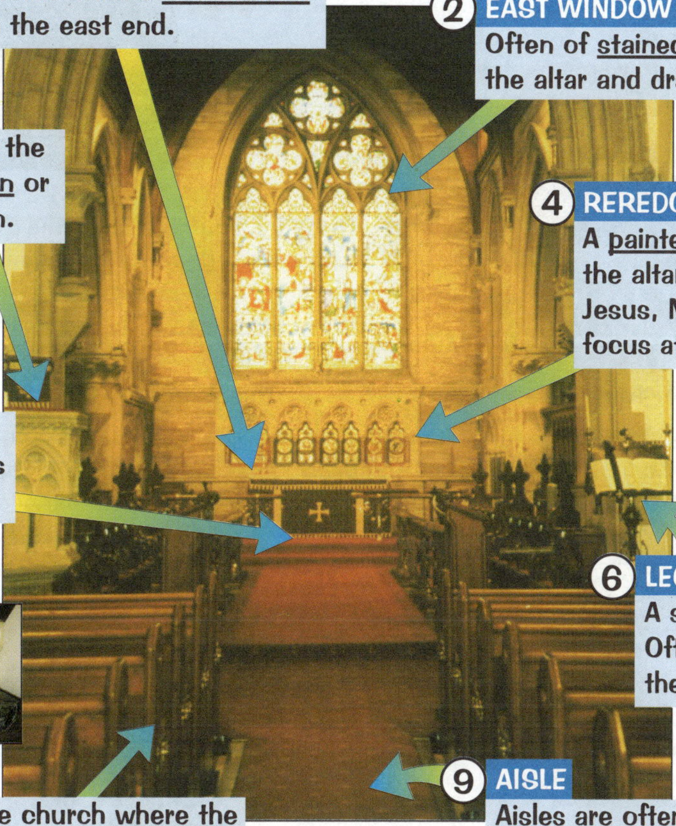

① **ALTAR**
The most important place in the church — a table which holds the items for the Communion service. The altar is in the east end.

② **EAST WINDOW**
Often of stained glass, it's right behind the altar and draws attention to it.

③ **PULPIT**
A raised box from which the minister gives the sermon or talks to the congregation.

④ **REREDOS**
A painted or sculpted screen behind the altar. Often has pictures of Jesus, Mary or saints. Helps to focus attention on the altar.

⑤ **SANCTUARY**
A raised platform where the most important parts of a service take place.

⑥ **LECTERN**
A stand for the church bible. Often made from brass in the shape of an eagle.

⑦ **COVERED FONT**
Used to hold holy water for Baptism.

⑧ **NAVE**
The main part of the church where the congregation sits (or originally stood).

⑨ **AISLE**
Aisles are often used in processions.

1) Roman Catholic, Orthodox and most Anglican churches use liturgy (see page 60) — where the focal point of the building is usually the altar — but there will also be a pulpit, lectern and pews (benches).
2) In Methodist, Baptist and United Reformed churches, there will be no altar, but a very large pulpit reflecting the centrality of the word of God. There will be pews or chairs.

A Church isn't used just for Religious Services

Okay, a church is a religious building — but it often has a more general use in the local community as well. Make sure you learn the kind of things a church is commonly used for:

RELIGIOUS SERVICES — Especially on Sundays, but also during the week. (Evensong is the name given to daily evening prayers.)

SPECIAL SERVICES — E.g. baptisms (christenings), confirmations, weddings, funerals, memorial services.

RELIGIOUS FESTIVALS — E.g. Christmas, Easter, Whitsuntide (Pentecost), Harvest Festival.

COMMUNITY USE — E.g. fêtes, talks and lectures, coffee mornings, playgroups and youth clubs, Scouts, Guides, and so on.

PARISH COUNCIL — Sometimes used for meetings and fund-raising events.

Weddings, funerals, Hugh Grant films...

Ah... pretty pictures. My mum took them. Anyway — the point of this page isn't to show off my mum's photography — it's to help you remember all the features of a typical church, and why they're important.

Religious Symbolism

Symbols are used within the Christian tradition to represent what's believed.
An obvious example is the symbol of the cross — used to represent the sacrificial death of Jesus Christ.

Religious Architecture is often Symbolic

1. Cathedrals can be enormous, demonstrating their importance. Like parish churches, they were historically built at the centre of the community to represent God's kingship on Earth. Inside, the focus of attention is always towards the altar, where the main act of worship (the celebration of Holy Communion) takes place.

2. Orthodox churches are often in the shape of a cross, with a large dome on top symbolising Christ's presence, eternity and the nearness of heaven. Inside they are richly decorated with friezes and carvings.

3. Free Churches (e.g. Baptists) meet in simple halls where the pulpit is the focus of attention. This shows the importance to them of preaching from the Bible. Also in a Baptist church, the prominence of the Baptistry (a pool for baptism by total immersion, see page 63) shows the central importance of baptism.

Icons, Statues and Stained-Glass Windows are Symbolic

1. Icons are paintings (mostly of saints) often found in Orthodox churches, and are often greeted with a kiss on entering the building. They're used to represent the presence of saints, and as a means to pray — 'prayers captured on wood'.

Statues also represent the presence of the saints.

In certain festivals a madonna (a statue of Mary) or another saint is paraded through the streets as an appeal to bless the community.

2. Large cathedrals and churches are often decorated with colourful murals or frescoes, and many feature beautiful stained-glass windows depicting biblical stories.

For centuries the finest work of leading artists was made for churches — all to offer to God the highest expression of worship, and to create a sense of awe.

Church Music is also Symbolic

Church music is symbolic as it is used to praise God and to express belief. Mozart, Bach, Beethoven and many other great composers wrote music for worship — e.g. Handel's Messiah, Mozart's Requiem Mass...

1. Hymns have been part of Christian worship for many centuries — they're often derived from passages of scripture.

2. In Protestant churches, choirs have an important role leading the singing. There are many types, from Anglican schoolboys to Pentecostal gospel.

3. Many different musical instruments are used in worship — from pipe organs to brass bands and guitars. The music used in worship can be solemn and dignified or loud and lively depending on the type of church.

4. Dancing is common in Charismatic churches — it's a sign of the Holy Spirit's presence.

Who sang that duff note? — hymn...

Don't forget that Christian beliefs are commonly expressed through worship in ritual form (e.g. baptism), and that this is also a kind of symbolism. There's also a link between religious symbolism and spirituality (see page 1). Oh yes, this stuff is all good fun, and a whole lot more interesting than maths. So there.

Revision Summary

All the stuff in that chunk of book should be meat and drink if you're going to get anywhere with the Christianity part of your RS Exam. Think about it... how do expect to be able to answer an Exam question about Christianity if you don't know the basic Christian beliefs... And believe it or not, that Jesus fellow is quite central to Christianity, so it makes sense to know a little about him (yes, even if you're not studying any of the Gospels modules). So learn, learn, learn away... and then try these questions. And keep trying them until they seem as easy as eating a nice big pepperoni pizza with extra cheese and mushrooms. And then go and buy yourself a nice big pepperoni pizza with extra cheese and mushrooms.

1) Describe 6 basic Christian beliefs mentioned in the Apostles' Creed.
2) What do Christians mean when they call Jesus 'the Christ'?
3) What does the term 'Incarnation' mean to Christians? What about 'Holy Spirit'?
4) Explain how the self-sacrifice of Jesus is relevant to Christians today.
5) Name the 2 major parts of the Christian Bible.
6) Explain 4 different ways of interpreting Scripture.
7) Write out the 10 Commandments from memory.
8) Name and define the 4 types of love according to the ancient Greek language. Which of these is a guiding Christian principle?
9) What is also needed before you can love somebody, according to Christianity?
10) What 5 things might Christians base their moral decisions on?
11) Describe 6 things that Jesus talked about during his 'Sermon on the Mount'.
12) Why do Christians think it is important to talk to non-Christians about their faith? What is the 'Great Commission' in Christianity?
13) What's the difference between absolute morality and relative morality?
14) What is meant by 'witnessing for Christ'?
15) Explain the 3 vows taken by someone adopting the monastic life of renunciation.
16) Explain what is meant by 'the Church' in Christianity.
17) What is the Communion of Saints?
18) Describe 2 ways in which the Church can claim to be influential.
19) Give 5 ways in which the Church might be active in a typical community.
20) What are the 3 main traditions (branches) of the Christian religion?
21) Write down 3 distinctive beliefs of the Roman Catholic Church which are not shared by Protestants.
22) Describe: a) the Charismatic Movement, b) Liberation Theology.
23) Explain each 'rank' of the Roman Catholic hierarchy.
24) What is meant by ordination?
25) Who is the head of the Anglican Communion of Churches?
26) What is the name given to the head of the Orthodox Church in a particular country?
27) In what way is the location of a parish church often symbolic?
28) In what direction are Christian churches traditionally aligned?
29) What is the function of:
    a) a church tower, b) a lych gate, c) a church's west door?
30) What is consecrated ground?
31) Where in a church does Holy Communion take place?
32) What are the following:
    a) the pulpit, b) the font, c) the nave, d) the lectern?
33) Describe 5 ways in which a church is used by the local community (these uses don't have to be religious).
34) Give 3 ways in which religious architecture is often symbolic.
35) What are icons? What is their significance in Orthodox churches?

Sunday Worship

Christianity grew out of Judaism, so Jesus would have kept Saturday as the Sabbath. However, Christians soon made Sunday their special day.

Sunday is 'The Lord's Day'

Sunday could have been made special for one of the following reasons:

1) Jesus rose from the dead on a Sunday.
2) It was a Sunday when the Holy Spirit visited the disciples at Pentecost.
3) Christians wanted to distinguish themselves from the Jews, though at first both Saturday and Sunday may have been regarded as holy by Christians.

1) The Roman Emperor Constantine adopted Christianity as the legal religion of the Roman Empire, and it was he who made Sunday an official day of rest — he even forbade town-dwellers to work on Sundays.
2) Few Christians today feel there should be a law requiring people to observe the Sabbath, but most see the value of devoting one day each week to God and to their families.
3) However, the 'Keep Sunday Special' campaign seeks to ban sport and non-essential work on a Sunday.

Sunday Worship in Church can take Many Forms

1) The exact form of Sunday worship will vary between denominations.
2) Most churches have their main service on a Sunday morning. It may be structured or spontaneous, but virtually all denominations use hymns or songs, Bible readings, and a sermon.
3) In Roman Catholic, Orthodox, and most Anglican churches it will be structured and liturgical (i.e. it will follow a pattern laid down in writing — with set prayers, and readings).
4) Methodists and other nonconformists have structured but non-liturgical services, e.g. following the 'hymn sandwich' pattern, where the service consists of hymns alternating with readings and a sermon.
5) Roman Catholic and Orthodox Sunday services always include Holy Communion (called Mass in the Roman Catholic tradition), and Anglican churches usually do.
6) Pentecostals, House Churches and other independent Christian fellowships may have spontaneous, often charismatic worship (see page 54).

There are several reasons for all this variety. Christians share the same basic beliefs about the importance of Holy Communion, the Bible, the sermon, the Holy Spirit etc., but they differ as to which matters most.

Holy Communion remembers the Last Supper

1) At the Last Supper, Jesus said that the bread and wine on the table represented his body and blood. The disciples were to eat and drink in remembrance of him whenever they ate together.
2) Roman Catholics believe in transubstantiation (i.e. the bread and wine used at Mass become the flesh and blood of Christ), and every Mass is a re-enactment of Christ's sacrifice (see also page 54).
3) Any leftover consecrated bread and wine must be consumed by a priest, or placed in a ciborium (a lidded chalice) inside a 'safe' called a tabernacle.
4) Many nonconformists simply regard Communion as a memorial service, and the Salvation Army and Quakers do not have Communion at all.

A Roman Catholic Mass or Anglican Eucharist will include the following:

i) Penitential Rite — confession of sin and absolution from it.
ii) The Liturgy of the Word — readings, sermon (called Homily by Catholics), creed, prayers.
iii) The Eucharistic Prayers — the priest consecrates the bread and wine using the words of the Last Supper.
iv) The Rite of Communion — the Lord's Prayer is recited and the bread and wine distributed.

A creed is a brief summary of religious beliefs.

On discovering that he had to eat the leftovers, Father Donald quickly made the switch to Communion pizza.

I'd like a hymn and mustard sandwich please...

There are a fair few names for Holy Communion, e.g. Mass, the Sacraments, the Eucharist, the Lord's Table, the Lord's Supper, the Breaking of Bread, and so on. You have to know everything about it. So there.

Christian Festivals

According to the Bible, no time of year is any more sacred than any other. However, certain times of year are used by Christians to commemorate, give thanks and celebrate specific aspects of their faith.

Christian Festivals Occur Throughout the Year

ADVENT — November / December

Advent marks the beginning of the Christian year, and begins 4 Sundays before Christmas. It's a period of preparation for Christmas and for Christ's Second Coming. Advent candles are lit in homes and churches, and Advent calendars may be used by children to count off the days until Christmas. Orthodox Christians observe 40 days' penance (showing true sorrow for sins).

CHRISTMAS — December 25th

Christmas celebrates the Incarnation — when God's Son came to Earth as a human being. We don't know the exact date of his birth, but we celebrate on December 25th. Customs vary around the world, but often date from pre-Christian times (e.g. Christmas trees). In many RC and Anglican churches there is a 'Midnight Mass' to welcome Christmas Day, and a crib (nativity scene).

Father Christmas Fact: Father Christmas used to be skinny and wear blue clothes, but started wearing red when he was used in Coca-Cola adverts.

EPIPHANY — January 6th

Epiphany commemorates Jesus being shown to the wise men, and his baptism and first miracle (turning water into wine at Cana). It marks the end of the '12 days of Christmas'. Decorations are taken down, and the transfiguration may be remembered.

When Jesus' clothes became a dazzling white, and he appeared to 3 disciples to be talking with Elijah and Moses.

LENT — February / March

Lent celebrates the 40 days and nights of Jesus' fasting in the wilderness after his baptism. The day before Lent is called Shrove Tuesday, a day for being 'shriven' (absolved from sin). Rich foods should be eaten up. Mardi Gras carnivals may be held ('carnival' means 'farewell to meat'). On Ash Wednesday (the first day of Lent) ash is put on believers' foreheads to show they are sorry for their sins. Few Christians today fast during Lent, but many still give up certain luxuries. Lent ends on the day before Easter.

HOLY WEEK — March / April

This is the final week of Lent, lasting from Palm Sunday (the Sunday before Easter, recalling Jesus' triumphal entry into Jerusalem — some churches distribute palm crosses) until the day before Easter. It commemorates Jesus' final week on Earth. Maundy Thursday recalls the Last Supper, and Good Friday Jesus' crucifixion. There are special services, especially on Good Friday between noon and 3pm — the hours when Jesus was dying on the cross.

EASTER SUNDAY — March / April

This commemorates Jesus' resurrection. Special services are held. Roman Catholics and some Anglicans hold an Easter Vigil beginning at midnight on the Saturday. Orthodox Christians gather outside their church until midnight, when the doors are flung wide and they file into a church flooded with light.

ASCENSION & PENTECOST — May / June

Ascension (40 days after Easter Saturday) marks the day when Jesus returned to his father in Heaven. Pentecost (or Whitsun) remembers the subsequent 'Coming of the Holy Spirit' upon the disciples (when they 'spoke in tongues'), empowering them to go out and spread the message of God's Kingdom — this is 50 days after Easter Saturday.

ASSUMPTION OF THE BLESSED VIRGIN MARY — August 15th

Roman Catholic and Orthodox Christians don't believe that Jesus' mother Mary died a normal death — instead she's believed to have been taken directly up to Heaven. This doctrine is not in the Bible, so Protestants don't accept it. In the Mediterranean world there is feasting and dancing, along with lavish procession and fireworks.

Some Catholic and Orthodox Christians observe saints' days too — in theory, every day of the year celebrates something.

Holy Days or holidays — who cares...

Because there are Christians all over the world, there's huge variety in the way festivals are celebrated. Many customs are cultural rather than Christian (e.g. Easter bunnies). Make sure you learn what the festivals celebrate and why, rather than how things are done.

Private Prayer and the Sacraments

Christian prayer is a conversation with God, and should take place both in church and in private.

Private Prayer draws a Believer Closer to God

The whole point of prayer is for the believer to draw close to God to communicate with him and hear what he's saying. Different Christians use different methods to accomplish this:

The 'Quiet Time' — time spent alone with God, perhaps reading the Bible and praying.

Meditation — a form of prayer where the believer clears his or her mind of distracting thoughts and concentrates on God's nature or work. It may involve repeating a prayer over and over again.

Contemplation — true Christian contemplation is not merely deep thinking — it's intimate wordless prayer in which the believer senses God's presence strongly.

The Rosary — used by Catholics, this is a string of beads arranged in groups. As the beads are moved through the fingers, prayers are said, e.g. the Lord's Prayer, Ave Maria (Hail Mary) and Gloria.

Icons — Orthodox Christians use icons (sacred pictures of saints) to help them focus on God. Although they may light a candle in front of the icon or kiss it, they don't pray to it.

Many parents pray with their children, believing this encourages them to grow up as praying Christians. And many Christians believe praying while ill helps them accept their suffering as part of God's plan.

The Seven Sacraments — Vehicles of God's Grace

Roman Catholic and Orthodox Christians believe in Seven Sacraments, through which they claim that God can communicate his grace (i.e. his 'saving energy') directly. The sacraments are:

1. **Baptism** Baptism or christening marks a person being officially accepted as a Christian.
2. **Confirmation** In this ceremony a Christian renews the vows made on his or her behalf at baptism.
3. **Reconciliation** This involves confession of a sin, followed by contrition, penance and absolution.
4. **Eucharist** In taking Holy Communion the believer receives Christ into him or herself afresh.
5. **Ordination** This is the rite in which people are made deacons, priests or bishops.
6. **Marriage** When a couple are joined in Holy Matrimony they receive a special blessing.

See pages 20 and 21 for more about marriage.

This is when a priest applies consecrated oil.

7. **Anointing of the Sick** This may be for healing, or to prepare a dying person for his or her journey into the next life, when it's also called extreme unction or viaticum.

Most Protestants accept only baptism and Eucharist as sacraments.

God is thought to communicate his grace directly through sacraments, whether or not the recipient understands what it all means.

Nonconformists generally regard baptism as a symbol — not a sacrament.

Fasting and Pilgrimage — Not Vital in Christianity

1) There are no longer any compulsory fasts for Christians, or special foods they must eat or avoid.
2) Festival foods (e.g. Christmas pudding, hot-cross buns) tend to be more cultural than religious in origin.
3) There are no compulsory pilgrimages either, although many like to visit the Holy Land (Israel). Catholics may also visit Rome, or places where the Virgin Mary has been seen — like Lourdes, or Knock.
4) They may make these pilgrimages to seek healing, or to deepen their faith.

Big Cats Rarely Eat 'Orrible Maggoty Apples...

Try this way of remembering the initial letters of the Seven Sacraments. It's a good 'un.

Baptism

Ritual bathing to symbolise purification or conversion was already practised by Jews.
The word 'baptism' comes from the Greek 'baptizo' meaning 'dip in water'. Not a lot of people know that.

Baptism Symbolises the Washing away of Sin

1) In the Gospels, John the Baptist (Jesus' cousin) instructed people to 'repent and be baptised'. Jesus himself was baptised by John (Mark 1:9-11), but John objected to this, saying Jesus should baptise him.
2) After the Resurrection, Jesus told his followers to "*Go and make disciples of all nations, baptising them in the name of the Father, Son and Holy Spirit.*" — Matthew 28:19. This is known as the 'Great Commission'.
3) Baptism symbolises a new life and the washing away of sin. A baptised person is sometimes said to be born again.
4) Christians are baptised in nearly all denominations except the Salvation Army and Quakers.

Roman Catholic, Orthodox and many Anglican Christians regard baptism as a sacrament (see page 62).

Baptism — meant for Infants or Believers...

Adults can be baptised in any denomination, if they haven't already been baptised as babies.

1) Those who regard baptism as a sacrament see no problem with baptising infants. They believe that this cleanses the baby from original sin, giving it a fresh start in life and making it a member of God's family.
2) Traditionally infant baptism was especially important if the baby was sick and likely to die — unbaptised babies were thought to be unable to enter Heaven.
3) Baptist, Pentecostal and House Church Christians, plus those from independent fellowships, tend to receive dedication as babies, and baptism only as believers. They believe you shouldn't be baptised until you are old enough to say you accept Christianity yourself.

In the Early Church, it tended to be adults who were baptised, though whole families (including children) could be baptised too.

Baptism Services can be Pretty Varied

Infant Baptism

1) Parents and godparents make promises on the child's behalf, which the child will later renew (if he or she chooses) at confirmation.
2) A sign of the cross is made on the baby, and holy water is poured three times over the forehead (in the name of the Father, Son and Holy Spirit), though Orthodox Christians baptise babies by total immersion.
3) The baptism is conducted over a font, and the baby is usually dressed in a white robe called a chrisom (white is the colour of purity).
4) A lighted candle may be given to parents and godparents to remind them of their duty to bring the light of Christ into the baby's life.
5) At the age of 7, Roman Catholic children have a special service of First Communion.

Believer's Baptism

1) This can take place in a church, a lake, a swimming pool, or even a skip. Several people are usually baptised at one special service.
2) Each candidate is asked questions about his or her faith, and may explain how and why he or she decided to become a Christian. He or she is then baptised by the minister by total immersion.

Baptism — an immersing topic...

Loads of information there — you need to know a) what baptism is, b) why it's important, c) why some people do/don't agree with baptising children and d) some of the common baptism rituals. Get stuck in.

Funerals, Burial and Cremation

Christians don't believe that only Jesus could be resurrected — they claim that they will be resurrected too. Which is possibly very good in a number of ways, but only if you don't have to do more exams. (And see page 11 for more on Christian beliefs about death.)

"Whoever believes in me will never die"

This is how the Christian Church sees death and resurrection:

1) Human beings sin, meaning that they don't live up to God's perfect standard. Because of this, they're not fit to be accepted into Heaven.
2) But Jesus broke the power of sin and death — his power and goodness were so great that after he was crucified, death could not keep hold of him. Jesus conquered it, both for himself and for his followers.

"I am the Resurrection and the Life. He who believes in Me will live, even though he dies; and whoever lives and believes in me will never die." John 11:25-26

See also page 45 for more about Jesus' resurrection.

Funeral Services are Sad, but with a note of Hope

Funeral services vary according to denomination, but all Christian funerals contain a note of hope. For many this doesn't mean wishful thinking — it means confident expectation based on God's promises.

1) The coffin is carried into the church, and the above verses from John 11 are often read. There are hymns, other Bible readings and prayers. The priest (or someone else) often gives a short sermon about Christian belief in life after death, and may also talk about the life of the person who has died.
2) Of course there will be sadness too, particularly if the person died young or very suddenly. There are prayers for the bereaved, and members of the congregation will express their sympathy for the family and close friends of the deceased. Black clothes are often worn, though some Christians consider this inappropriate and may even request guests not to dress in this way.
3) It doesn't matter whether the body's buried or cremated — Christians believe that at the Resurrection they will have new 'spiritual bodies', not their old ones. There's usually another short service at the graveside or crematorium, then afterwards often a meal for family and friends.

Roman Catholic Requiem Mass

A Roman Catholic funeral includes Holy Communion (the 'Requiem Mass'). The purpose of a Requiem Mass is to pray for the soul of the dead person. The priest wears white vestments, and the coffin is covered with a white cloth (a pall). The coffin is sprinkled with holy water and the priest says, *"In the waters of baptism (name) died with Christ, and rose with him to new life. May s/he now share with him in eternal glory."* The coffin is later sprinkled again, and also perfumed with incense.

Funeral Customs help Support the Bereaved

1) Christian funeral services have a great deal to say about the hope of eternal life. The bereaved person is encouraged to believe that one day she or he will be reunited with the deceased.
2) In the days following the funeral, family and friends often try to contact those who were closest to the deceased, and encourage them to talk through their grief.
3) Usually the priest or vicar will also try to visit, and may offer counselling, or suggest someone who can. There are several stages to the process of grief, and it can help to talk to someone who understands this.

Hmm... Perhaps a bit premature...

Don't talk to Buffy about life after death...

Phew — depressing way to end the section. But Christians try not to see death as depressing — after all, they believe the person who died is going to Heaven (probably), which has to be a good thing, if you're a Christian. Of course, it'd be a bit of a downer if you thought they might go to Hell, but let's not dwell on that.

GOSPEL

Jesus and Mark's Gospel

Christianity sees Jesus as the Son of God — and so his story is pretty important.

The Gospels — Good News, but Not Biographies

See page 46 for more about the Gospels.

1) Three of the Gospels (Matthew, Mark and Luke) are very similar, and are called the Synoptic Gospels.
2) The Early Church believed that all 4 Gospels in the New Testament (the Synoptic Gospels, plus John) were written by apostles, or by men who had known the apostles well — this is how they got their authority.
3) They quickly established their place as Scripture (holy writings inspired by God).

There's a lot of Uncertainty surrounding the Gospels

1) The Gospels were written to preserve the story of Jesus after the apostles died, but they also pointed to the future coming of the Kingdom of God, and answered questions that the early Christians were asking.
2) An early Christian wrote that Mark was the 'interpreter of Peter', but that he hadn't known Jesus personally. Mark may have used early collections of Jesus' words and actions, or he may have got information from Peter. (See pages 69 and 70 for more about Peter.)
3) It's accepted that Mark's Gospel was probably written in Rome between 65 and 75 CE — partly to encourage Christians who were facing persecution from the Emperor Nero.
4) It's probably impossible to work out the story of Jesus' life exactly. But since Jesus was Jewish, he will have been circumcised, and educated in the Torah and other Jewish literature and traditions. He will have visited synagogues, observed the Sabbath, and gone to Jerusalem for the 'Pilgrim Festivals'.

The Gospels tell the Story of Jesus

All references are to Mark's Gospel.

In the Gospels, Jesus is called by a number of titles, each of which gives a clue as to who he is/was.

SON OF GOD

No person uses this title until after Jesus' death. It was blasphemous to Jews.

i) At his baptism (1:9-11) a voice comes from Heaven saying, 'You are my own dear Son.'
ii) At the transfiguration (9:2-8), when Jesus' clothes become a dazzling white and he's seen talking to Elijah and Moses, a voice from a cloud says, 'This is my own dear Son: listen to him.'
iii) At the Trial before the High Priest (14:53-65) the High Priest asks, 'Are you the Messiah, the Son of the Blessed God?' and Jesus answers 'I am.'

SON OF MAN

The prophet Daniel (Daniel 7:13-14) talks about a 'Son of Man' who would have great authority from God.

This title is the one which Jesus uses when referring to himself. It symbolises the fact that Jesus felt ordinary human emotions. It's also used by Jesus to claim the authority mentioned by Daniel.

i) Jesus uses it when healing the Paralysed Man (2:1-12) — he says, 'I will prove to you (the teachers of the Law) that the Son of Man has authority on earth to forgive sins.'
ii) In response to the Request of James and John to sit at Jesus' side in his glory (10:35-45), Jesus says, 'The Son of Man did not come to be served, but to serve, and to give his life as a ransom for many.' James and John have not understood the nature of Jesus as a Messiah.
iii) In his Prediction of the Passion (8:31-33), he says, 'The Son of Man must suffer much and be rejected... he will be put to death but 3 days later he will rise to life.' Jesus seems to see himself as the kind of 'suffering servant' prophesied in Isaiah 53:2-12.

CHRIST, MESSIAH, SON OF DAVID

Christ and Messiah mean 'anointed one', and it's a woman at Bethany who anoints Jesus by pouring perfume over his body. Although Jesus saw himself as the Messiah, he wasn't what most Jews were expecting. Many expected a warrior king, or a prophet like Moses.

i) At Caesarea Philippi (8:27-30) his immediate followers recognise Jesus as the Christ.
ii) Blind Bartimaeus (10:46-52) is the first person to acclaim Jesus as Son of David in public without being told to shut up.
iii) During Jesus' Entry into Jerusalem (11:1-11), the crowd cheers, 'Blessed is the coming of our Father David'. (See page 72 for more about David.)

SAVIOUR

'Jesus', 'Yeshua' and 'Joshua' all mean 'Saviour'.

i) The Calming of the Storm (4:35-41) and the Feeding of the 5000 (6:30-44) show Jesus controlling nature and providing miraculous food to save his people from harm.
ii) In healing the Syro-Phoenician woman's daughter (7:24-30), Jesus demonstrates that his salvation can extend to Gentiles (i.e. non-Jews) as well as Jews.

This stuff is true — it's all gospel, mate...

And see page 46 for different ways of interpreting the Bible — especially the Gospels.

GOSPEL

The Kingdom of God

The 'Kingdom of God' ('Kingdom of Heaven' in Matthew) was a key element in Jesus' teaching. Christians believe that when Jesus began his ministry, God's Kingdom arrived on Earth.

The Kingdom of God — there are Two Sides

Jesus uses the phrase in his first and last major speeches:

1. At the outset of his ministry, Jesus went into Galilee proclaiming the good news of God.

   "The time has come. The Kingdom of God is at hand. Repent and believe the good news." — Mark 1:14-15

2. At the Last Supper:

   "I will never again drink this wine until the day I drink the new wine in the Kingdom of God." — Mark 14:25

There are 2 sides to the Kingdom of God — i) it has already begun...

Many Jews had expected the Kingdom to arrive spectacularly and undeniably, along with the Messiah. This is why the Pharisees asked Jesus when the Kingdom of God would come (Luke 17:20). Jesus' answer was, "*The Kingdom of God is within you.*" (Luke 17:21). He may have meant that God's Kingdom was already in people's hearts, but that most of them were preventing its growth.

...and ii) it is still to come.

He also taught that when the final judgement comes, all those who accept God as King will be in the Kingdom. Those who have not accepted him will be outside the Kingdom. But at Jesus' Second Coming the Kingdom would be spectacularly revealed "*...like lightning, which flashes and lights up the sky...*" (Luke 17:22-37).

The Kingdom — Conditions for Entry

Jesus and the Children (Mark 10:13-16)
To enter the Kingdom, Jesus said that you must accept it like a little child (i.e. with open trust and gratitude, rather than an adult's cynicism).

The Rich Young Man (Mark 10:17-27)
Jesus told a young man to give away all his property and follow him — he said it was desperately hard for a rich person to enter the Kingdom, although everything is possible for God.

"It is easier for a camel to go through the eye of a needle, than for a rich man to enter the Kingdom of God."

Jesus tell Loads of Parables about the Kingdom

These are a few of the parables of the Kingdom of God in Marks' Gospel.

The sower (4:3-20)
Hearers of the Gospel are like types of soil — seed only grows in good soil. Similarly, the word of God will only flourish in a person if they live a 'Kingdom of God' lifestyle.

The growing seed (4:26-29)
The Kingdom grows gradually but there's no stopping it.

The mustard seed (4:30-32)
It's very small to start with, but ends up enormous.

The tenants in the vineyard (12:1-12)
A man leaves his vineyard in the hands of tenants, and sends various messengers to collect the rent — but all are killed by the tenants. They even kill the man's son so the vineyard will become theirs. Instead the owner kills the tenants and gives the vineyard to others. This parable is told to the high priests and Pharisees — they are compared to the tenants who would kill the man's son for their own ends. The vineyard owner represents God.

The patches and the wineskins (2:21-22)
Jesus says that no one patches old clothes with a new patch, or pours new wine into old skins. This is about Jesus' way being completely new — it's not merely an update of old stuff.

Parable of the lamp (4:21-25)
You bring a lamp in to make things visible. Jesus is the lamp — he is to help people see the new way.

This should separate the sheep from the goats...

A parable is an easy-to-understand story that parallels a real-life situation — a bit like the 'Hare and the Tortoise'. Or like that one my old history teacher used to tell about a dachshund that doesn't revise for his dachshund exams and subsequently fails miserably. But I dunno what that one was supposed to parallel.

GOSPEL

Jesus and Miracles

Jesus performs many miracles in the Gospels. He performs them basically for two reasons — to show that he has God's power, and to demonstrate the importance of faith. (All references are to Mark's Gospel.)

Jesus Controls Nature — inspiring Awe and Wonder

Jesus calms the storm (4:35-41)
A storm breaks out and threatens to sink the boat Jesus and the disciples are in. Jesus calmly instructs the wind to die down, which it does. The disciples are filled with awe at what they see.

Jesus feeds the 5000 (6:30-44)
A crowd has gathered around Jesus and the disciples, but there are only 5 loaves and 2 fish to eat. Jesus gives thanks to God, breaks the bread and the disciples pass the food round. All 5000 people have enough to eat, and there's enough food left over to fill 12 baskets.

Jesus walks on water (6:45-52)
Jesus catches up with his disciples' boat by walking across the water. Although they have seen him feed the 5000, they are still shocked at his powers.

Jesus Cures Mental Illness — but Faith is Important

A man with an evil spirit (1:21-28)
While teaching in the synagogue, a man shouts, "What do you want with us, Jesus of Nazareth? Have you come to destroy us?" Jesus sees the man is possessed by an evil spirit and says sternly, "Come out of him!" The spirit shakes the man violently, but comes out of the man with a shriek.

A man with evil spirits (5:1-20)
A man called Legion is possessed by so many evil spirits that he is able to break the chains on his hands and feet. Jesus sends the spirits into 2000 pigs instead, who rush down to the lake and drown themselves. Jesus tells the man to spread the word about what he has done.

The Syro-Phoenician woman (7:24-30)
A non-Jewish woman begs Jesus to drive the evil spirit from her daughter. Jesus tells the woman that the 'children' (i.e. Jews) must be 'fed' first — meaning his healing powers are intended for Jews. She argues that surely the 'dogs' (i.e. non-Jews) can have the scraps the children don't want. For this answer, Jesus heals her daughter. She has faith that Jesus' power is for everyone, even though she doesn't get an instant response.

The boy with an evil spirit (9:14-29) (see page 68)

Jesus Heals Physical Illness — and Challenges Beliefs

Jesus heals a man with a dreaded skin disease (1:40-45)
Jesus tells him to keep the story to himself, but the man immediately tells many people, making Jesus more well known.

Jairus' daughter (5:21-42) (see page 68)

Jesus heals a paralysed man (2:1-12)
A paralysed man is brought to Jesus. Jesus forgives the man for his sins. The crowd think that only God can forgive sins, and accuse Jesus of blasphemy. Jesus asks whether it is easier to forgive sins or cure a paralysed man. The man then gets up and walks, proving the Son of Man has authority to forgive sins on Earth.

Jesus heals the haemorrhagic (5:25-34) (see page 68)

Jesus heals a deaf mute (7:31-7)
He commands the amazed onlookers not to talk about it. But the more he tells them to keep quiet about it, the more they talk about it.

The man with the paralysed hand (3:1-6)
Jesus cures a man with a withered hand in a synagogue on the Sabbath — this goes against the Pharisees' teaching. Jesus looks at them and asks, "*Which is lawful on the Sabbath: to do good or to do evil, to save life or to kill?*" The Pharisees' stubbornness angers and distresses Jesus.

The blind man at Bethsaida (8:22-25)
Jesus cures a blind man by spitting on and touching his eyes. He then tells the man not to go into the village.

For goodness' sake — make your mind up...

Although Jesus sometimes wants to keep news of his miracles from spreading, at other times he seems to want people to spread the word. It's hard to work out why he wanted the miracles kept secret (but see page 69 for one idea), and just as hard to see why he changed his mind. I don't know... these Messiahs.

GOSPEL

Miracles, Faith and Conflict

The Gospels teach that faith, prayer and commitment are all needed if you want to enter the Kingdom of God. Jesus demonstrated them consistently in his own life, and encouraged his followers to do the same.

Miracles and Faith are Linked

Jesus exercised his own faith every time he performed a miracle. And he showed that people could be cured miraculously of both physical and mental illness — as long as they had faith. (See also page 67.)

JAIRUS' DAUGHTER (Mark 5:21-24, 35-43)
Jairus, a synagogue official, begs Jesus to heal his daughter. When Jesus arrives, the girl is apparently dead already, but Jesus revives her. As in most of the healing miracles, faith is crucial. Here the sick girl's father has demonstrated faith on her behalf (by asking Jesus for help).

This also shows that not all important Jews were against Jesus.

THE BOY WITH AN EVIL SPIRIT (Mark 9:14-29)
The disciples attempt to cure a boy with an evil spirit (some say the boy was epileptic, but who's to say...). When they fail, Jesus says to the father that the boy can only be healed if he shows faith. The father says he has faith, but not enough. Jesus then casts the evil spirit out, and says that 'only prayer can drive this kind out'.

It's also made clear in this story that he expects his followers to perform healings and exorcisms, just as he does himself.

The point of all these stories is to show the importance of faith.

THE WOMAN WITH A HAEMORRHAGE (Mark 5:25-34)
While Jesus is on his way to Jairus' house, a woman with severe bleeding touches his cloak in the crowd. She is healed, even though Jesus says he does not know who has touched him. He tells her that her faith has made her well.

1) In these stories, faith is not merely a passive 'belief in God' — it is active, and involves taking a 'step of faith' in the direction you believe God is leading, and expecting God to intervene as a result.
2) So in the 'Boy with an Evil Spirit' story above, the boy's father claims to have 'faith but not enough' (i.e. faith mixed with doubt). But because he exercises the little faith he has, his son is healed.

In Mark 6:1-6 (Rejection at Nazareth), Jesus can hardly perform any miracles because the people didn't have faith — so the faith of the people he dealt with seems just as vital as his own relationship with God.

Conflict — Jesus Challenges 'Pointless' Traditions

The Pharisees were a group of influential Jews that applied the various religious rules very strictly. Jesus wasn't afraid to challenge them, even though he knew it would be dangerous.

All references are to Mark's Gospel.

Paying taxes (12:13-17)
Jesus avoids the trap of some Pharisees and Herod's men when they ask him who to pay taxes to — Caesar or God. *"Give to Caesar what is Caesar's, and to God what is God's."*

See also 'The man with the paralysed hand' (3:1-6) on page 67.

Ritual washing (7:14-23)
The Pharisees have elaborate laws about washing before eating. Jesus argues that what a man does makes him unclean, not what he takes in, and says the Pharisees are more concerned with their own traditions than God's word.

Picking corn on the Sabbath (2:23-7)
The Pharisees accuse the disciples of working on the Sabbath when they pick ears of corn. Jesus reminds them that David (see page 72) ate on the Sabbath, and that "*the Sabbath was made for man, not man for the Sabbath*".

George Michael too, said, "You gotta have Faith"...

The passages from Mark's Gospel on this page are only examples of stories where faith, prayer and commitment are important. There are others, but these ones are in the 'got to know' category. And make sure you know how Jesus challenged authority when he felt it was necessary. It's important stuff.

Discipleship

GOSPEL

These are the lessons of discipleship, as told in Mark's Gospel.

The Call of the Disciples — Jesus Gathers his Followers

Call of the disciples (1:16-20)
"Come, follow me, and I will make you fishers of men."

Jesus gathers his 12 Disciples.

The word 'disciple' means 'follower', and is often used to refer to one of Jesus' 12 followers from the Gospels. But it can also be used more generally to mean any Christian.

Mission of the 12 (6:7-13)
Jesus sends his disciples out with authority over evil spirits. They are to take a staff — but should not take bread, money, a bag or an extra coat. Where they are made welcome, they are to stay in that place until they leave town. Where they are not made welcome, they are to shake the dust from their feet as a marker to others.

The calling of Levi (2:13-17)
Jesus has dinner at Levi's house with people the Pharisees call 'sinners'. Jesus says that healthy people don't need doctors — meaning his role is to save 'sinners'. (Note: Levi wasn't one of Jesus' 12 disciples from the Gospels.)

Peter expresses his faith at Caesarea Philippi (8:27-30)
Jesus asks Peter (one of his disciples) how he describes Jesus when people ask. "*You are the Christ,*" replies Peter. Jesus tells his disciples not to tell anyone about him.

Discipleship — there are Duties and Rewards

The Duties and Qualities of a Disciple

A follower of Jesus must:

...love children (9:37)
"Whoever welcomes one of these little children in my name welcomes me; and whoever welcomes me does not welcome me but the one who sent me."

...be faithful in marriage (10:11-12)
Jesus taught that anyone who divorces and remarries is committing adultery.

...be for Jesus
"Anyone who is not against Jesus is for Jesus." (9:40)

...be servant of all (10:43)
"...whoever wants to be first must be slave of all."

...take up their cross (8:34)
"If anyone would come after me... he must deny self and take up his cross and follow me."

...be willing to make sacrifices (The widow at the treasury) (12:41-44)
While many rich people make large offerings at the treasury, a widow gives only two small coins. Jesus says her offering is greater, as it is all she had to live on.

...preach the Gospel (The Commission) (16:14-18)
After his resurrection, Jesus gave his disciples their mission... He urges them to preach the Gospel, saying whoever believes will be saved, but whoever does not will be condemned. And in Jesus' name they will "*drive out demons; they will speak in new tongues; they will pick up snakes with their hands; and when they drink deadly poison, it will not hurt them at all; they will place their hands on sick people, and they will get well*".

The Rewards for a Disciple

But it's not all hard work. There's some good news too...

True Family (3:31-35)
"Whoever does God's will is my brother and sister and mother."

Rewards of discipleship (10:28-31)
Whatever you give up now, you'll get a hundred times as much, both now and in the future, i.e. you may face persecution now, but there is eternal life in the end.

Discipleship — is that the one that Jesus walked on water to...

At Caesarea Philippi Jesus tells the disciples not to tell anyone about him — maybe Jesus doesn't want to become too famous too soon. This secrecy is also in some (but not all) of the stuff on page 67, and is known as the Messianic secret. And have a look on page 68 for stories of conflict.

Jesus' Trial and Death

GOSPEL

It's a fairly famous story... you may just know something about this already.

The Last Supper — Jesus knows he will be Betrayed

1) During the Passover meal, Jesus says that one of the disciples will betray him — each disciple denies it will be him.
2) Jesus breaks a piece of bread and says, "*Take it; this is my body.*" He passes round a cup of wine and says, "*This is my blood of the covenant, which is poured out for many.*"
3) Jesus also foresees that Peter will deny him three times — something that Peter refuses to believe.

Jesus says about the disciple who will betray him, "It would be better for him if he'd never been born."

He is Arrested, Tried and Crucified

1) Jesus and the disciples go to Gethsemane. Jesus is fearful of death, but vows to do as God wishes.
2) Jesus' betrayer arrives — it is Judas. He has come with an armed crowd, and has arranged a secret signal with them — the person he kisses is the one they should arrest. He kisses Jesus, who goes with the crowd.
3) Jesus is put on trial before the Sanhedrin (the Jewish religious court). Various priests and elders testify falsely against Jesus, but their stories don't agree with each other.
4) Eventually, the high priest asks Jesus, "*Are you the Christ?*" Jesus answers, "*I am, and you will see the Son of Man sitting at the right hand of the Mighty One on the clouds of heaven.*" This is enough for them to condemn Jesus for blasphemy.
5) In the courtyard below, Peter is accused of being a follower of Jesus. He denies it twice... but then remembers Jesus' prediction. He breaks down and weeps.
6) Jesus is turned over to Pilate — as the governor, he has the power to sentence Jesus to death. But Jesus answers none of the questions Pilate asks, to Pilate's amazement.

7) Pilate is to release a prisoner to mark Passover, and he lets the crowd choose who they want — they can have Jesus or Barabbas, a murderer. But the high priests have primed the crowd to shout for Barabbas... Jesus is flogged, and handed over to be crucified.
8) The Roman guards mock Jesus — they make him a crown of thorns and pretend to honour the 'King of the Jews', while all the time hitting and spitting at him.
9) Jesus is led to Golgotha, where he is to be crucified. Simon of Cyrene is made to carry his cross.
10) Jesus refuses the drugged wine he is offered, and is then crucified next to two robbers. A sign is fixed to Jesus' cross that reads "The King of the Jews". Passers-by and the Roman soldiers throw insults at Jesus, saying that he can work miracles, but he can't save himself.
11) Before dying, Jesus cries out, "*My God, My God, why have you forsaken me?*" As he dies, the curtain of the Temple is torn in two, and a Roman soldier remarks, "*Surely, this man was the Son of God!*"

And then he's Resurrected

1) Mary Magdalene, Mary the mother of James and Salome go to Jesus' tomb, only to find that Jesus has gone. A young man there says they are to spread the word among the disciples. The two women flee in terror.
2) Jesus appears first to Mary Magdalene. She passes the news on to the disciples, who refuse to believe.
3) He then appears to the disciples and rebukes them for not believing in his resurrection. He orders them to preach the Gospel, and perform miracles in his name.
4) Jesus then ascends into Heaven and sits at the right hand of God.

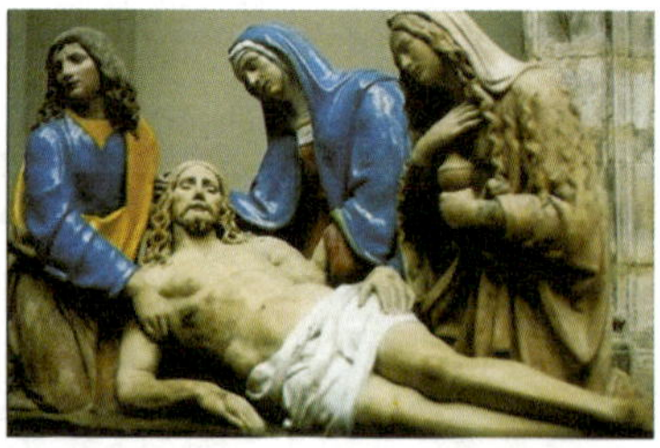

The examiners won't be impressed if you don't know this...

Like I said, it's a fairly famous story, but you need to be able to describe in detail all the events of Jesus' death and resurrection — and I mean all of them. Or you could wait until Easter and watch that series they made a few years ago, with that famous bloke in. But then you can't watch James Bond.

Revision Summary

Yes, indeed it's that time again. The good old revision summary to check you haven't been sleeping through the last 10 pages. I know what you're thinking — "I could just... skip... it." But you can't, do you hear? You CAN'T! There's no way you could possibly remember all the facts from this section first time through — so use these questions to fill in the gaps. Come on, how bad can it be...

1) Explain why Sunday might have become a special day for Christians.
2) Choose 2 contrasting denominations and describe a typical Sunday service for each.
3) Explain how Holy Communion originated.
4) What do Roman Catholics mean by the word 'transubstantiation'?
5) Make a list of Christmas customs practised in the UK. Which of these are specifically Christian?
6) What do the following Christian festivals celebrate:
   a) Epiphany, b) Ascension, c) Pentecost?
7) Write down from memory the names of the Seven Sacraments.
8) Why might a Christian go on a pilgrimage?
9) What does baptism symbolise?
10) Why do some denominations not believe in baptising newborn babies?
11) Describe a typical Christian funeral service.
12) Explain how Christian funeral customs seek to help a bereaved person cope with his/her loss.
13) When was Mark's Gospel probably written?
14) What are the 4 titles given to Jesus in Mark's Gospel?
    For each title, name 2 occasions when it is used.
15) What did Jesus mean by the phrase 'Kingdom of God'?
16) Write about 2 passages in which Jesus speaks about entering the Kingdom of God.
17) Explain the following parables of the Kingdom of God:
    a) The sower, b) The tenants in the vineyard, c) The parable of the lamp.
18) Describe 3 miracles that show Jesus controlling nature.
19) Describe another 3 miracles that show Jesus curing mental illness.
20) And another 3 miracles that show Jesus curing physical illness.
21) According to the Gospels, what is the connection between faith and miracles?
22) Jesus wasn't afraid to challenge the Pharisees. Describe 3 occasions when he did this.
23) Describe 5 duties of being a disciple of Christ. What is a disciple's reward?
24) Describe the events of the Last Supper.
25) Describe the story of Jesus' arrest, trial, death and resurrection.

The Beginnings of Judaism

If you're asked to explain the origins of Judaism, remember that there was more than one founder. In fact, there are 3 key figures you should know about:

Abraham (between 2000 and 1800 BCE)

1) Jews call him Avraham Avinu ('our father Abraham'). He was the first of the patriarchs — the founders of Judaism.
2) Unlike his neighbours in Ur, he believed in one god. God told him to leave Ur and go to Canaan, also known as The Promised Land, The Holy Land, and later Israel. God promised this land to his descendants.
3) God made a covenant with Abraham (see below) — this covenant forms the basis of Jewish beliefs.

The time since the birth of Jesus is known as the 'Common Era' (CE), and BCE just means 'Before the Common Era'.

Very often, 1800 BCE is written 1800 BC (Before Christ).

And 2002 CE (Common Era) is often written AD 2002.

Moses (around 1300 BCE)

1) Abraham's descendants had to leave Canaan and escape to Egypt because of a famine.
2) In Egypt they multiplied and the Egyptians made them slaves for 400 years.
3) Moses then led them to freedom — an event called the Exodus. Their journey back to Canaan took 40 years.
4) On the way back, Moses received the 10 Commandments and the rest of the Torah (meaning 'Instructions', or 'Law') at Mount Sinai.
5) Moses is regarded as the greatest of the prophets, and is known as Moshe Rabbenu ('our teacher Moses').
6) Moses' successor Joshua led the reconquest of Canaan.

David (not long after 1000 BCE)

1) For a long time the Israelites lived in Twelve Tribes under warlords called Judges.
2) Unfortunately, the tribes made a dangerous enemy, the Philistines, that the judges couldn't really do anything about.
3) So the tribes asked God for a king, and got Saul.
4) Saul's successor, David, captured Jerusalem from its pagan inhabitants and made it his capital. He reigned for 40 years and created a small empire.
5) David's son Solomon built the first permanent Jewish temple in Jerusalem.
6) After Solomon the kingdom split in two. The 10 northern tribes were soon swallowed up by Assyria. The 2 southern tribes together became known as Judah, and Jews are descended from them.

This Temple has been destroyed a couple of times, but is still very important in Judaism.

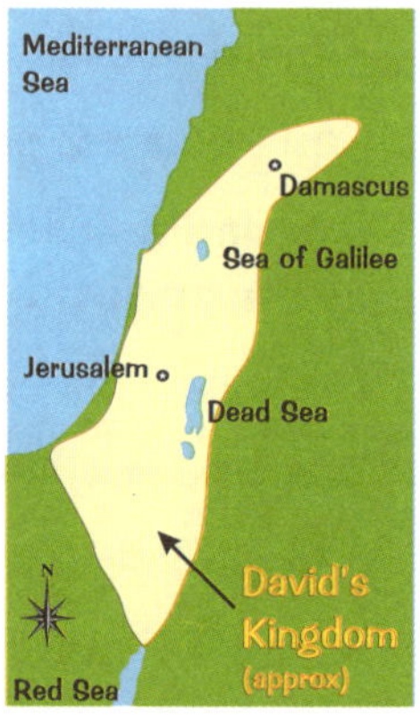

The Covenant — Key to the Past and Hope for the Future

1) Jews think that their relationship with God is like a two-way promise (a covenant).
2) God made a covenant with Abraham, where God promised Abraham many descendants that he would never abandon. In return they had to be circumcised.
3) The covenant was renewed at Mount Sinai with the giving of the Torah.
4) Jews regard their history as the story of the covenant. Some things described in the covenant haven't happened yet — these are believed to describe the future.
5) Jews look forward to the Age of the Messiah ('anointed one'), when all of Israel will belong to them and a new age of universal peace will dawn.

Learn this page — and be as wise as Solomon...

There's a lot more to RS than knowing facts — but at the same time, you can't get far unless you actually know them. Without facts you're left with holy waffle. This impresses no one — least of all examiners. So write the 4 subheadings on a page, then list the important facts underneath them — all from memory.

Basic Jewish Beliefs

Jews don't all believe exactly the same things. They have many different opinions on many important issues. But most Jews share some basic beliefs about their God, themselves and their land.

"Hear O Israel: the Lord our God, the Lord is One"

Most Jews believe these 11 things about God. They believe God is...

Belief in one god is called monotheism.

- **...ONE** — Jews believe there's only one God. The heading above comes from Deuteronomy 6:4 — it's the opening of a very important Jewish prayer called the Shema.
- **...A PERSON** — i.e. he's not just a 'force' like the one in Star Wars, but neither is he an old man with a beard. Human beings were made 'in his image' (but this needn't mean he looks like us).
- **...THE CREATOR** — i.e. he made the Universe and everything in it. Jews don't invent clever arguments for God's existence — they say that creation makes it obvious that he's there.
- **...THE SUSTAINER** — i.e. he didn't just create the Universe and then sit back — his energy keeps it going.
- **...HOLY** — 'Holy' means 'set apart' or 'completely pure'. God (or YHWH in Hebrew) is so holy that some Jews won't even write or say the word 'God' — they write G-d and say Hashem ('the Name') or Adonai ('the Lord', or 'the Master').
- **...OMNIPOTENT** — i.e. all-powerful — although he still allows each person free will.
- **...OMNISCIENT** — i.e. he knows everything, even your smuttiest secrets and your wildest dreams.
- **...OMNIPRESENT** — i.e. present throughout the whole Universe.
- **...THE LAWGIVER** — Jewish tradition says 'God wrote himself into the Torah'.
- **...THE TRUE JUDGE** — Jews believe they shall all face him one day, for death is not 'the end'.
- **...THE REDEEMER** — Jews believe God is merciful. He will save his people from sin and suffering.

See also pages 6 and 9.

Jews Believe they are a Chosen People

1) Because of the covenant, Jews believe they have a special role to play in history.
2) But they believe they were chosen for responsibility, not for privilege — God wanted people who would dedicate themselves to him, and prepare the world for when all human beings would come to know him.

Israel is the Holy Land

Zionism (after Zion, one of the hills on which the holy city of Jerusalem was built), is the belief that the Jews should have a homeland of their own — the land God gave them.

1) The Jews lost their homeland in the 6th century BCE, when much of the population of Judah was taken into exile in Babylon (although many returned in 5th century BCE).
2) Later, the Jews suffered conquest by the Greeks, and then by the Romans. After a rebellion in 70 CE, the Romans destroyed Jerusalem.
3) For many centuries most Jews had to live abroad — this time is known as the diaspora. It was only after 6 million died in the Holocaust during the Second World War that the state of Israel was established.
4) For many Jews the establishment of the State of Israel in 1948 heralded the fulfilment of the Zionist dream. But others disagreed, for two main reasons:

> 1) It seemed wrong to displace the Palestinians who were living there. There was likely to be violent opposition to Jewish settlement. And indeed there was — and still is.
> 2) Some Jews believed it was the job of the Messiah to restore the Jews to their homeland. God's people should have waited for him to come, rather than putting their trust in corrupt politicians.

The examiner's got his Zion you — so learn this well...

You might get asked about how these beliefs could affect a person's life. For example, if God created everything, shouldn't we respect and protect the environment? And if God is omniscient, does that mean my old history teacher was God — he seemed to know everything. No, his name was Mr Davis. My mistake.

Sources of Guidance

The 'Jewish Bible' is the Tenakh. This is basically the same as the Christian Old Testament, except that it's in a different order. The letters in the word 'TeNaKh' even help you remember the order of its groups of books.

The Tenakh — its Letters tell you its Contents

T = Torah (Instructions / Law / Teachings)

The Torah is the first five books of the Bible (Genesis to Deuteronomy). It contains 613 commandments (mitzvot) which Jews are supposed to live by. Jews regard the Torah as the holiest part of the Tenakh, as it was given to Moses directly by God.

N = Nevi'im (Prophets)

This collection of books is divided into two. The Former Prophets trace the history of the Israelites after the death of Moses. The Latter Prophets contain the words of Isaiah, Jeremiah, Ezekiel and 12 Minor Prophets. All these men encouraged the Jews to keep their part of the covenant, and their words are believed to have been inspired by God. However, the books in the Nevi'im do not have as high a status as the Torah.

K = Ketuvim (Writings)

This is a hotch-potch of other stuff, chiefly the three 'P's: Psalms (hymns), Proverbs (wise and witty sayings), and Philosophy. This part of the Tenakh is less authoritative than the others.

Torah means Different Things to Different People

Some Jews use the word 'Torah' to refer to the whole Tenakh. Others use it to mean the enormous body of teachings which grew up over the centuries to explain how the Torah should be applied in a changing world. Although some of these teachings were originally passed on by word of mouth (and were known as the Oral Torah), they eventually they got written down in a number of collections — you need to know the names:

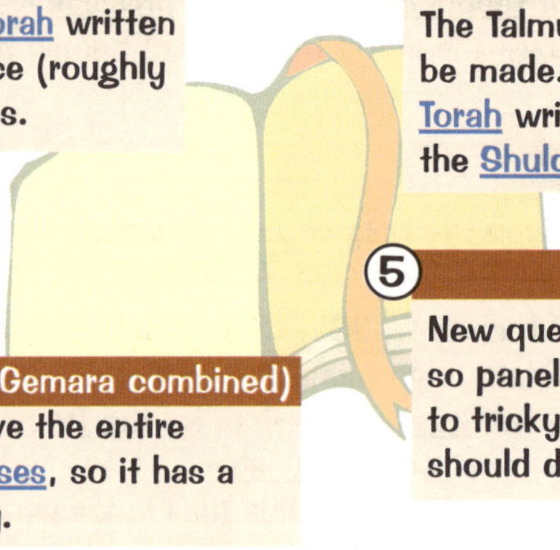

1 The Mishnah ('Learning' or 'Repetition')

This was a collection of Oral Torah written down by Rabbi Judah the Prince (roughly 200 CE). It ran to 63 volumes.

2 The Gemara ('Completion')

This is an extended commentary on the Mishnah.

3 The Talmud (the Mishnah and Gemara combined)

Some Jews think that God gave the entire contents of the Talmud to Moses, so it has a very high status and authority.

4 The Codes

The Talmud was so huge that summaries had to be made. An important example is the Mishneh Torah written by Maimonides in 1167. Another is the Shulchan Aruch from the 16th century.

5 The Responsa

New questions arise as technology develops, so panels of rabbis meet to give 'responses' to tricky questions, e.g. whether people should drive on the Sabbath.

The Bet Din is a Rabbinical Court

1) A Bet Din has three judges (dayasim), who rule on issues which remain unclear (in spite of the huge amount of other guidance available).
2) Individual Jews can approach the Bet Din to sort out legal or business disputes. It also supervises kosher food products and divorces.

The word 'Halakhah' describes Jewish Law as a whole. It means 'going' — in other words, how to 'walk with God' the Jewish way. It's the part of Jewish teaching which is concerned with ritual and behaviour.

Keep on studying and you'll soon get Tenakh of it...

Hebrew words can be spelt in different ways when written in our alphabet. If you see a word on your exam paper which looks unfamiliar, try pronouncing it in your head — it might make sense after all.
For example, you might see the word 'Tanach' — but it turns out this is just a different way to spell Tenakh.

The Holocaust

The word Holocaust means 'a complete burning up' or 'total destruction'. It refers to the massacre of six million Jews by the Nazis between 1933 and 1945. Jews also call it Shoah ('whirlwind').

The Holocaust — the Nazis' Extermination of Jews

1) Towards the end of the 18th century, Jews living in Europe began to face greater persecution than ever before from nationalists who thought that Jewish blood was watering down their own racial identity.
2) This hatred of Jews became known as anti-Semitism, and spread through many countries — especially France, Germany, Austria and Russia. The fact that many Jews regarded themselves as loyal citizens of these countries didn't stop this from happening.
3) Later, during the 1920s, Germany faced huge economic problems. The National Socialist (Nazi) Party seemed to offer solutions. It pinned the blame for the country's problems on 'non-Aryan' people (i.e. those who weren't considered 'pure Germans') living in Germany — especially the Jews.
4) In 1933 its leader Adolf Hitler became Chancellor of Germany, and laws began to be passed which gradually deprived the Jews of their citizenship rights.
5) Eventually Hitler introduced the Final Solution — the plan to wipe out the Jews completely. Throughout World War II (1939-1945) concentration camps and extermination camps were built in the countries under Nazi control. Huge numbers of Jews perished here in gas chambers.

The Holocaust caused Jews to ask "Where was God?"

The holocaust posed very serious problems for Jews — they had to find answers to questions like:

If God exists, and he is good, and all-powerful, how could he have allowed such terrible suffering?

If we are the 'chosen people' how could God have let six million of us be wiped out?

See pages 8 and 9 for more about religious questions of evil and suffering.

Holocaust Remembrance Day is 27 Nisan.

'Nisan' is the first month in the Jewish calendar.

Jewish Responses to the Holocaust have been Varied

Jews have come up with many responses to this type of question:

1) Some Jews have concluded that there is no God.
2) Some have concluded that if God does exist, he either doesn't care, or is powerless to intervene.
3) Some Jews say that the Holocaust, and all suffering, is a test of faith — if good people always got the best things in life, everyone would be good for the wrong reasons.
4) Some Jews say that God could intervene to stamp out evil if he chose to. However, he gave all human beings free will and refuses to override this even when it is abused. Also, it would be impossible for God to 'destroy all evil people' because no one is completely evil or completely good.
5) Some Jews regard all those who died in the Holocaust as martyrs for the faith, and see their martyrdom as 'sanctifying the name of God'.
6) Some say the most important thing is to keep practising Judaism, or else Hitler will have won.
7) Some have devoted their energies to building the State of Israel (established in 1948) so that Jews may never again be forced to live with persecution.
   But are they persecuting the Palestinians (see page 73)?

Six million people died in the Holocaust.

Six million people. Hard to comprehend.

Different Jewish Traditions

There are certain Jewish cultures and traditions that you need to be aware of.

Different Jewish Cultures are Described in Different Ways

1) Some Jews (known as 'secular Jews') don't practise their religion at all — they may not even believe in God. But they still regard themselves as Jews. To a Jew, if your mother's Jewish, then you're Jewish.
2) Sephardic Jews' ancestors lived for centuries in Spain, Portugal and North Africa (i.e. mainly in 'Muslim' countries).
3) Ashkenazi Jews lived in central and eastern Europe (mainly in 'Christian' countries).
4) The Sephardim and Ashkenazim differ in their customs, their way of pronouncing Hebrew, and in some of their prayers.

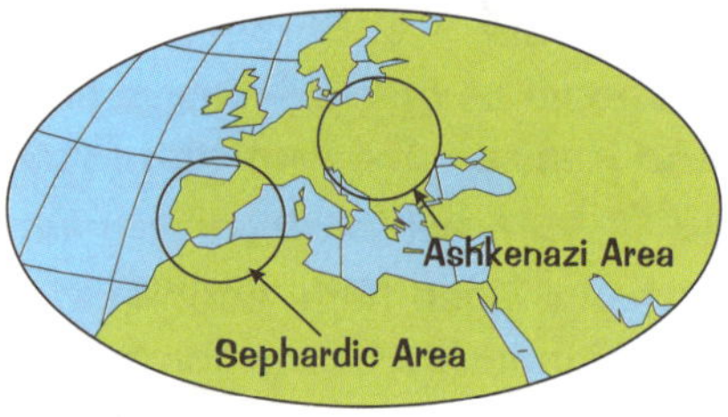

Orthodox Jews Live Strictly by the Torah

1) Orthodox means 'right belief'. Orthodox Jews accept that traditional Jewish beliefs and practices are still important today.
2) Roughly 80% of British Jews belong to Orthodox synagogues, though not all are equally observant.
3) Those who *are* observant believe that Progressive Jews (see below) have betrayed Judaism by watering it down and taking liberties with God's word.
4) Ultra-Orthodox Jews take their orthodoxy very seriously — some would say, to extremes. The most famous ultra-Orthodox group are the Hasidic Jews.

Hasidic Jews are ultra-Orthodox

1) Hasid means 'pious one'. The movement was started by Rabbi Israel Baal Shem Tov in 18th century Poland (and most Hasidim still dress in 18th century Polish style).
2) Baal Shem Tov believed in keeping every word of the Torah strictly — but also with joy and enthusiasm.

Progressive Jews Interpret the Torah Less Rigidly

1) Progressive Jews apply the Torah to modern life in a very different way.
2) Progressive Jews believe that the Torah is merely people's interpretation of the word of God.
3) They consider the moral commandments binding (although open to interpretation).
4) However, the ritual laws can be adapted or abandoned in response to changes in society.
   In Britain, there are 2 Progressive movements: Reform and Liberal.

Reform Judaism

1) Reform Judaism began at the end of the 18th century, when Jews in Europe were allowed to take a full part in society.
2) The first reformers tried to update synagogue services by making them more like Christian ones.
3) Reform Jews stopped praying for the restoration of the Holy Land and the rebuilding of the Temple (see page 72). They also gave up believing in the physical coming of a Messiah — instead they hope for a Messianic Age of universal peace.
4) They allow women a much greater role in worship — men and women sit together in services, and there are women rabbis. Also, modern languages are used in worship — not just Hebrew.

Liberal Judaism

1) Liberal Judaism was founded at the start of the 20th century.
2) The originators thought that even Reform Judaism was too strict.
3) They taught that observing any mitzvot is a matter of personal choice.

The Masorti movement (Conservative Judaism) tries to take a middle way, between Reform and Orthodox Judaism.

What's the difference between a non-observant Orthodox Jew and a Progressive Jew?

Neither of them obeys the Torah, but the Orthodox one feels guilty about it.

Reform Judaism — No, I think it's okay as it is...

Not all Jews look the same, believe the same things, or live in the same way. The differences described on this page fall into two basic categories: geographical differences (e.g. where in the world your ancestors came from), and differences in beliefs (e.g. secular, orthodox or progressive).

Judaism and Day-to-Day Life

Observant Jews believe that their day-to-day lives should be lived in a way which is pleasing to God. For Orthodox Jews this means obeying the 613 mitzvot in the Torah, covering everything from sex to seafood.

Mitzvot means Commandments

The most famous mitzvot are the Ten Commandments (see page 47) — but they're not the only ones. The 613 mitzvot can be divided up in different ways...

248 of the mitzvot are positive, telling Jews what they should do.
365 are negative, telling them what they shouldn't be doing.

Ritual mitzvot are about Jews' relationship with God.
Moral (ethical) mitzvot are about Jews' dealings with other people.

The first four of the Ten Commandments are ritual mitzvot, and the last six are moral mitzvot.

The singular of mitzvot is mitzvah.

1) Orthodox Jews believe that the commandments given by God are his chief method of communicating with his people. Their method of responding is obedience.

2) They also believe that living God's way is in their own best interests. They reason that if God is our Maker, and the Torah is the 'Maker's Handbook', it makes sense to follow its guidance. Deuteronomy 10:12-13 says, "*Keep, for your own good, the Commandments of the Lord.*"
3) There's also a belief that observing mitzvot causes people to lead disciplined lives, which in turn builds character.
4) Progressive Jews take a rather different view. They think the Torah is God's teaching as interpreted by human beings. Therefore mitzvot which no longer seem relevant can be adapted or even abandoned.

Morality Matters in Judaism

1) Observant Jews think it's vital to live by a moral code, and will generally regard a moral individual as someone who combines religious observance with concern for other people.
2) In deciding how to behave, Jews look first to the Torah, then to the Talmud, then to the wider body of traditional Jewish teaching. But an individual Jew can always ask someone who knows more about these things than they do.
3) Jews realise that no one can live by all 613 mitzvot all of the time. But they believe that God is merciful and will always forgive someone who is truly sorry for his sins. Rosh Hashanah and Yom Kippur (see page 83) remind Jews of this every year.

The word 'mitzvah' is sometimes translated as a 'good deed'. Doing anything to help a fellow human being is pleasing to God.

The Mikveh is a Ritual Bath — used for 'Family Purity'

1) A mikveh is a ritual bath. It should be a special tiled pool about 3-5 metres long and 2-3 metres wide, and contain rainwater.

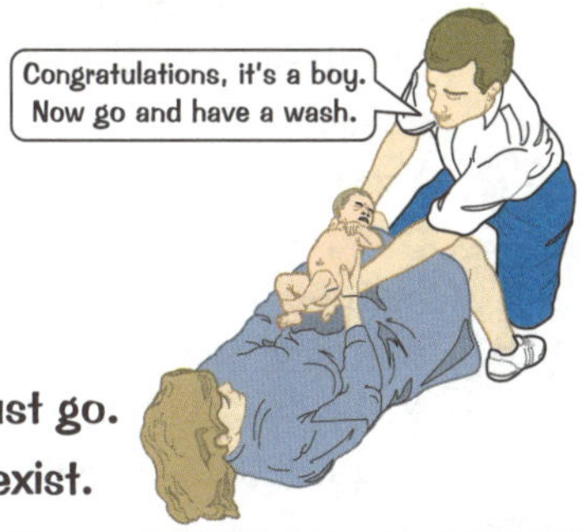

2) Traditionally, Jews immerse themselves in a mikveh to be purified from 'spiritual uncleanness'. The mikveh isn't about getting rid of a bit of dirt — Jews have to shower before entering the mikveh.
3) Women should visit the mikveh after menstruation, before marriage and after childbirth. Men go in preparation for Yom Kippur. All converts to Judaism must go.
4) Progressive Jews tend to reject the use of the mikveh as old-fashioned and sexist.

That's an awful lot of rules...

Wow — 613 rules covering everything you do during the day. That reminds me of something, but I can't think what... yep, I've got it now... I was thinking of school. Anyway, as long as you learn all the stuff on this page, as well as all the stuff in the rest of the book, I'm sure you'll be fine in the Exam.

The Synagogue

A Jewish place of worship is called a synagogue, although Jews more often use the word 'shul', or sometimes even 'Bet ha Knesset' (House of Meeting).

It's not what's on the Outside that matters...

There are no rules stating what a synagogue should look like on the outside — they can be plain or ornate, traditional or ultra-modern. But you might recognise a synagogue from symbols on its outside walls, such as a menorah (a seven-branched candlestick), or a magen David (a six-pointed star/shield of David).

...it's what's on the Inside that's Important

The layout of the synagogue's Prayer Hall is based on that of the ancient Temple. It faces Jerusalem, where the Temple stood, and is usually rectangular. All synagogues share the following four features:

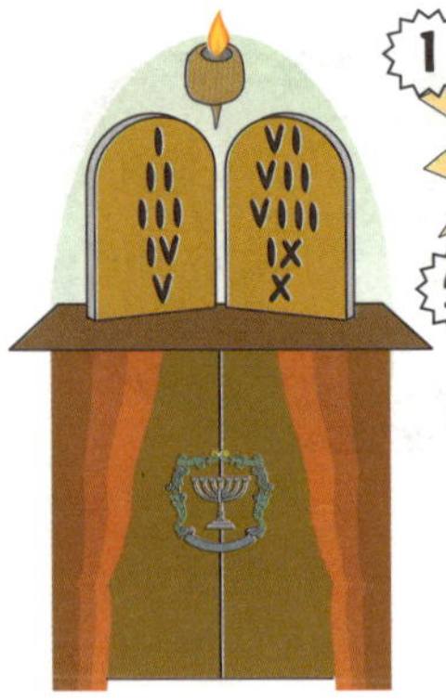

1. Aron Hakodesh (the Ark) — this is the most important item of furniture. It is a large cupboard or alcove, with doors or a screen, set on the wall facing Jerusalem.
2. Ner Tamid (Perpetual Light) — above the ark is a light which never goes out. It represents the menorah which was always kept alight in the Temple.

Remember — there will be no 'pictures of God'.

3. Sefer Torah (Scrolls of the Torah) — parchment scrolls. On each end is a wooden pole for winding it to the required passage. It must be handwritten by a sofer (scribe), and is usually decorated. They're kept inside the ark.
4. Bimah or Almemar — a raised platform with a reading desk, normally in the centre of the hall.

Also, some synagogues have a pulpit, and the Ten Commandments above the ark. Some have an organ (but on the Sabbath, all singing should be unaccompanied), and an Orthodox synagogue will have a gallery where women can sit.

... and how it is Used

A synagogue is a bit like a community centre. In addition to the Prayer Hall, a synagogue will have a hall for wedding receptions and parties, classrooms for study groups, a mikveh perhaps (see page 77), plus rooms for youth clubs, mother and toddler groups, senior citizens' clubs, and so on.

The Most Important Officials — the Rabbi and the Chazan

THE RABBI

1) Every synagogue has a rabbi (meaning 'my master'). To become a rabbi, you have to study for many years and have practical training.
2) The rabbi's role is much like that of a minister in a Christian church — he leads prayers in the synagogue, conducts weddings and funerals, visits the sick, and may be chaplain to a hospital or prison.
3) But rabbis are not priests — Jews don't believe that anyone can mediate between an individual and God.

THE CHAZAN (CANTOR)

1) Many synagogues also have a chazan (cantor), specially trained in music and voice projection.
2) His role is to lead the congregation in singing. He chants some of the prayers on Shabbat, and at festivals, weddings and funerals.
3) He may also provide entertainment at receptions and parties.

Learn all this and you'll pass at a cantor...

If you're studying Judaism, you need to know about synagogues. There's just no getting away from that. It's like trying to get away with passing your maths exam without really getting to grips with what a 'number' is. Do I make myself clear... Do I? Good. I'll try to calm down now.

Signs and Symbols

Symbols: Visible Signs of Invisible Ideas...

Since God is invisible, symbols are important in just about every religion. Believers use symbols to help them focus on God in private prayer and in communal worship. A picture on a wall, a household object and an item of clothing may all be used as religious symbols.

But Jews have No Pictures of God

There are two reasons why Jewish art never tries to picture God.
1) No one knows what he looks like.
2) The 2nd of the 10 Commandments forbids it as idolatry.

"You shall not make for yourself an idol in the form of anything in heaven above or on the earth beneath." Exodus 20:4

Symbols in the Home: the Mezuzah

"These commandments that I give you today are to be upon your hearts... and you shall write them on the door-frames of your houses." Deuteronomy 6:6-9

1) The mezuzah is a sign which is put in Jewish houses.
2) It's a tiny parchment scroll containing the words of Deuteronomy 6:4-9 and 11:13-21 in Hebrew. It must be handwritten by a trained scribe, and is put inside a case to keep it safe.
3) There's one on the front door and every other door of the house except the bathroom and toilet. It constantly reminds the family of the covenant.

Ritual Dress is important in Judaism

Kippah (Yarmulka, Capel, Skullcap)

Many Jewish men and boys wear a small cap as a sign of respect to God. It reminds them that God's intelligence is vastly higher than ours. There's no actual law commanding men to cover their heads when praying, but it's an almost universal custom.

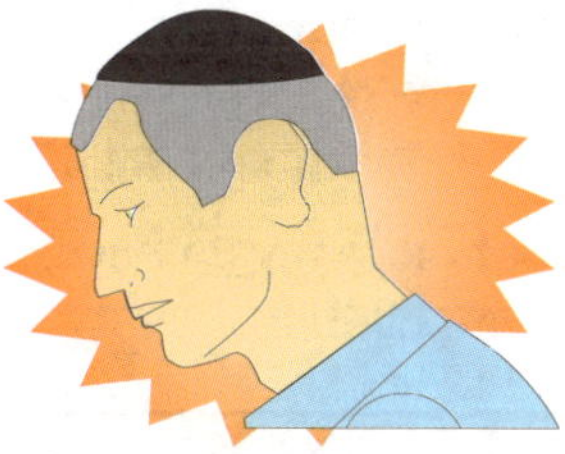

The Tefillin (Phylacteries)

These are worn during morning prayers, except on the sabbath and on festival days. They are 2 leather boxes, one worn on the upper arm (next to the heart), one on the head. Inside are tiny parchment scrolls containing 4 Bible passages: the first 2 paragraphs of the Shema (see page 6), plus Exodus 13:1-10 and 13:11-16. These remind Jews to serve God with head and heart.

The Tallit (Prayer Shawl)

This is also worn by males during morning prayers. It's a square or rectangle of silk or wool. Some Jews wear a 'tallit katan' (small tallit) all the time, under their clothes.

The Tzitzit (Fringes)

Fringes are attached to each corner of the tallit, in obedience to Numbers 15:37-41 and also Deuteronomy 22:12.

There's something fishy here — must be my kippah...

You need to know why these special clothes and symbols are important in Judaism. Learn what each thing represents, and how it's useful — e.g. ritual dress helps people stay focused while praying. It's a shame you can't get clothes to keep you focused (or awake even) while revising...

Judaism and Children

Rites of passage are ceremonies marking the transition from one stage of life to the next.
Like most religions, Judaism has ceremonies associated with birth, coming of age, marriage and death.

There are Three Important Birth Ceremonies

Brit Milah

1) This is the 'Covenant of Circumcision', and involves the removal of the foreskin from the penis (and so is only for boys). The baby boy is also named at this time, and afterwards there is a celebratory meal.
2) The circumcision is done when a boy is 8 days old, and is for religious rather than medical reasons. The operation is carried out in hospital, at home or in the synagogue by a specially trained 'mohel' while being held by the 'sandek' (often the grandfather).

Redemption of the First-born

Note: a modern rabbi isn't the same as an ancient priest.

Originally, all first-born boys became priests. Now, when a boy is 30 days old, his father ceremonially releases him from the priesthood by redeeming him (i.e. 'buying him back') with five silver coins.

The Naming of a Girl

Jewish girls usually receive their names on the Sabbath following their birth, although some Sephardic Jews name girls at a ceremony called zeved habat ('gift of a daughter') when they are 7 days old.

Children are Taught about Judaism in Different Ways

1) At home, parents might try to create a religious environment using symbols of the faith, and so on.
2) Children might go to the synagogue for Hebrew classes. And some children will attend Jewish schools, which teach Hebrew, Torah and Talmud as well as the normal curriculum.
3) Almost all festivals have features specifically designed to involve children.

At Pesach the youngest child asks questions about the festival.
And during the readings in the synagogue at Purim, the children drown out the name of the evil Haman with football rattles.

Bar Mitzvah and Bat Mitzvah are Coming of Age Ceremonies

Bar Mitzvah is for Boys

1) At 13 a boy becomes Bar Mitzvah (Son of the Commandment) and is responsible for keeping the mitzvot for himself. This is also when a boy begins to wear tefillin for prayer.
2) On the Sabbath after his 13th birthday there is a special service, followed by a small reception, and perhaps a lavish party (although not all Jews approve of such extravagance on a religious occasion).

Bat Mitzvah and Bat Chayil are for Girls

1) A girl becomes Bat Mitzvah (Daughter of the Commandment) at 12, since Judaism recognises that girls mature before boys. The ceremonies vary widely, but among Progressive Jews, Bat Mitzvah ceremonies may be exactly like Bar Mitzvah.
2) Many synagogues have a ceremony for 12-year-old girls called Bat Chayil (Daughter of Excellence). Girls prepare by studying their responsibilities as women, then make a short speech at a special service.

What's funny about Bar Mitzvahs then...

These rites of passage are important — they're important stages of a person's life, and things you're likely to remember. They're like doors opening to a new part of your life. You could compare them (sort of) to passing your driving test, or getting your first job. Nothing will be the same again.

Jewish Beliefs About Death

You need to know what Judaism teaches about death and the afterlife, and the rituals surrounding death.

The Souls of the Dead end up in Sheol

1) Most religious Jews believe in life after death, but as the Torah is very vague on the subject, they don't necessarily agree on what it will be like.
2) The Torah mostly talks about 'Sheol', a shadowy underworld where the souls of the dead end up.

3) According to Maimonides (see page 74), belief in the resurrection of the dead is one of the main beliefs in Judaism — when the Messiah comes, the dead will be raised to life, and to judgement.
4) Sheol is sometimes compared to Hell, but Jews don't believe in Sheol as a place of everlasting torment — it's more like a laundry where souls are cleaned up to make them fit for an eternity spent in the presence of God.

Judaism has Customs to Comfort the Bereaved

There are many rituals in Judaism concerned with death. They are designed to help bereaved people accept what has happened, give expression to their grief, receive comfort, and come to terms with their loss.

1. Jewish families gather together to be near a loved one who is dying, while the dying person should spend his / her last moments confessing sins and reciting the Shema (see page 6).
2. After the death, each member of the family makes a small tear in their clothing — a symbol of grief and shock.
3. The dead person must not be left alone, and must be buried (not cremated) as soon as possible, preferably within 24 hours.

It's the job of the Chevra Kaddisha (burial society) to prepare the body for burial.

4. The body's washed and put in a mikveh (see page 77). Then it's wrapped in a plain linen shroud, before being placed in a plain, unpolished, wooden coffin — in death rich and poor are equal.
5. At the funeral service in the synagogue, psalms are read and a prayer is said praising God for giving life and for taking it away. The rabbi might make a short speech about the deceased.

6. The first week after the funeral is called shiva (seven). The immediate family stay at home and are visited by relatives and friends who pray with them three times a day and offer comfort. They do not cut their hair, shave, listen to music or have sex. The men recite a prayer called the kaddish. Everyone is encouraged to talk about the person who has died.
7. The first month after the funeral is called Sheloshim (thirty). During this time life returns gradually to normal, and male mourners go to the synagogue to recite the kaddish. Anyone who has lost a parent remains in mourning for a whole year.
8. The anniversary of death is called Yahrzeit. It is on the first yahrzeit that the headstone will usually be erected above the grave. Every year a candle is lit for 24 hours and men say the kaddish.

Schole — where the soles of the dead end up...

All religions will have very strong thoughts on death generally, as it's one of those difficult times that people have always had to face, from the beginning of time basically. Judaism is no exception here. And it's worth checking out page 12 as well — there's more about death there, which might be handy to have a read of.

Jewish Prayer and the Sabbath

The Jewish holy day is the Shabbat (Sabbath), but in Judaism, prayer is important every day of the week.

There are Three Special Times for Daily Prayer

1) Prescribed daily prayers happen at 3 special times — evening, morning and afternoon.
2) At these times, men will try to attend the synagogue and become part of a minyan — a group of at least ten men, which is the minimum needed for a service. Women (traditionally because of their domestic commitments) are trusted to pray at home.
3) As well as the normal daily prayers, there are also special prayers for when getting up, going to bed, before and after eating... in fact, pretty much every event in life, good or bad, can be a reason to pray.

Shabbat (Sabbath) is Celebrated in the Synagogue...

The Sabbath is a day of rest to commemorate the 7th Day of Creation when God rested after making the Universe. It begins at sunset on Friday, and ends on Saturday evening when stars begin to appear.

There are 3 separate services in the synagogue on the Sabbath.

FRIDAY EVENING Shabbat is welcomed as a queen or a bride with singing led by a chazan (cantor). No instruments are used — in memory of the destruction of the Temple (see page 72) with its instrumental music.

> The 4th Commandment instructs Jews to observe the Sabbath.
> "*Remember the Sabbath day by keeping it holy.*" — Exodus 20:8

SATURDAY MORNING the main service of the week. The rabbi will read from the Torah and give a sermon. Also, seven men are called up to read or recite a blessing, and an eighth reads a portion from the Nevi'im. In Orthodox synagogues, women sit separately from the men and take little part.

SATURDAY AFTERNOON this service includes a reading from the Torah, and three special prayers.

...and in the Home

1) To prepare for Shabbat, the house is cleaned and tidied, and all the food to be eaten on Shabbat is cooked in advance. Family members bathe or shower. At dusk, the mother of the family will light two candles and welcome the sabbath by saying a blessing and gesturing with her arms.
2) At the beginning of the Shabbat meal, a sanctifying ceremony called kiddush takes place. It happens at home and at the synagogue, and includes the reciting of Genesis 2:1-3 (God resting after creation). Wine is used to symbolise the sweetness and joy of Shabbat.

> The Mishnah lists 39 kinds of 'work' not allowed on the Sabbath.

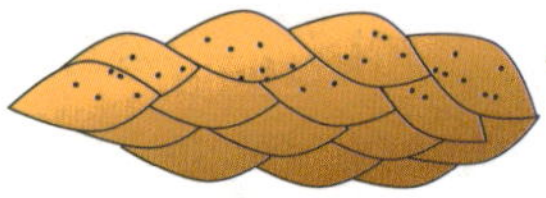

3) Challot are eaten — these are plaited loaves which commemorate the double portion of 'manna' which God provided the day before each Shabbat during the exodus. They are blessed, cut and dipped in salt.

4) After the father has blessed his children, the Shabbat meal is eaten.
5) The havdalah ('division') ceremony marks the end of Shabbat, separating it from the six days ahead. Blessings are said over sweet-smelling spices, a cup of wine, and over a special plaited candle.

This page must seem like manna from heaven...

Ho, ho, ho... Anyway, this page describes the behaviour of observant Orthodox Jews. Progressive Jews tend to have a more relaxed attitude to things like exactly when Shabbat should begin and end, and to prayer and worship generally. Also their women are permitted to take an equal part in worship with the men.

Pilgrimage, Food and Fasting

Prayer isn't the only way to worship in Judaism...

Pilgrimage — More than a Holiday

Pilgrimage is a way to show devotion to God, and is a symbol of spiritual quest.

1) Before the Romans destroyed Jerusalem in 70 CE, Jews from all over Israel were expected to go up to the Temple three times a year for the 3 Pilgrim Festivals — Pesach, Sukkot and Shavuot.
2) Today there are no compulsory pilgrimages for Jews to make, but diaspora Jews (i.e. those living outside Israel) often visit the Holy Land.

Three places are particularly important to pilgrims:

The Western Wall (aka the Wailing Wall)
This is all that remains of the Temple (see page 72). Here many Jews mourn its destruction, and place prayers in the wall's cracks.

Masada
This is a huge fortress in the Judaean desert. Here 1000 Zealots held out against the Romans from 70-73 CE. They eventually committed suicide to avoid being enslaved.

Yad Vashem (the Holocaust Memorial)
The names of the concentration camps are engraved in the floor of a candlelit hall.

Kashrut — the Jewish Food Laws

1) Observant Orthodox Jews follow a special diet based on the Kashrut (Jewish food laws).
2) Permitted food is called kosher — everything else is treifah ('torn').
3) These laws were not originally laid down for reasons of health or hygiene — they are an example of statutes from God to test Jews' obedience, and to mark them out as different from other nations.
4) To be kosher, a mammal must have cloven (split) hooves and chew the cud. Fish with fins and scales are kosher, but no other seafood is. Some birds are also kosher.
5) Animals and birds must be specially slaughtered with one cut across the throat using a razor-sharp blade. Blood must not be eaten, and meat and dairy products must not be eaten together. Foods that aren't meat or dairy may be eaten with either.

In Judaism, food is associated with happiness — so fasting shows grief or repentance.

Judaism teaches that true repentance can atone (i.e. make amends) for any past transgression — 'the gates of repentance are always open'.

The Days of Awe — Rosh Hashanah and Yom Kippur

These special days aren't really festivals — they're two stages in the process of judgement and atonement.

ROSH HASHANAH IS JEWISH NEW YEAR — it falls in the autumn.

1) It's believed that God judges his people for the year's misdeeds on Rosh Hashanah, and decides what their circumstances will be in the year ahead.
2) During the last month of the old year and on Rosh Hashanah itself, a shofar (ram's horn) is blown. The shofar expresses the crying out of the soul as it yearns to be reunited with God.
3) The tashlich ('casting away') ceremony also takes place — a prayer is said to ask God to remove the sins of his people. It should be said by the bank of a river.

Between Rosh Hashanah and Yom Kippur come 10 days of repentance.

YOM KIPPUR — THE DAY OF ATONEMENT

'Atonement' means making amends for wrongdoing.

Features include: a visit to the mikveh (ritual bath) the previous evening, fasting for 25 hours, the wearing of the kittel (white smock), chanting of the Kol Nidre ('annulment of vows') and the Neilah (closing service).

I'm telling you — this information's kosher...

By the time you've finished your revision, you'll have learnt quite a bit of Hebrew. Just make sure you learn Hebrew words carefully — there are sometimes variant spellings, but this doesn't mean that any old spelling will do. Stick to the spelling you've learnt. Lecture over — you can get back to your cup of tea now.

Jewish Festivals

These are the Jewish festivals you need to know about. So learn away...

Learn these Six Major Jewish Festivals

FESTIVAL	WHEN	TO COMMEMORATE	FEATURES AND FOODS
Purim (Lots)	Early spring	Esther, a Jewish girl who became Queen of Persia in the 5th century BCE, saving the Jews from being annihilated by Haman.	1) The day before Purim is a fast. 2) Reading of Megillah (scroll of Esther). 3) A football rattle is used to drown out the name of Haman. 4) Fancy dress and plays.
Pesach (Passover)	Spring	The exodus from Egypt — when Moses led the Israelite slaves from Egypt to freedom. In Egypt, the angel of death killed the first-born sons of the Egyptians, but passed over the Israelites.	1) Leaven (something that makes bread rise — yeast, for example) is forbidden. 2) Seder (Passover meal) with matzah (biscuit), wine, salt water, bitter herbs, karpas (a vegetable), burnt egg, bone.
Shavuot (Weeks)	Early summer	Giving of the Torah to Moses on Mount Sinai 7 weeks after leaving Egypt.	1) Synagogues are decorated with flowers. 2) Men study the Torah all night. 3) Cheesecake is eaten.
Sukkot (Tabernacles)	Autumn	The Israelites' trek through the desert with Moses, and the shelters (tabernacles) they camped in.	1) Family decorates and lives in a 'sukkah' — a temporary shelter. 2) Use of the '4 species': etrog (citron), lulav (palm branch), aravot (willow) and hadassim (myrtle).
Simchat Torah (Rejoicing of the Torah)	Autumn	End of the annual cycle of Torah readings (and beginning of the next one).	1) Synagogue readings from the end of Deuteronomy and beginning of Genesis. 2) Men take all Torah scrolls from the Ark (see page 78) and dance round the synagogue 7 times, singing and clapping.
Hanukkah (Chanucah) (Dedication)	Winter	Victory of the Jews over the Syrian Greeks under Antiochus Epiphanes (in the 2nd century BCE).	1) Special 8-branched candlestick called a hanukiah (chanuciah) is lit. 2) Doughnuts are eaten. 3) Children play with a spinning top.

A doughnut-eating festival — where can I sign up...

Make sure you can spell the names of all the festivals, and don't get mixed up about which one celebrates what. And don't forget about the 'Days of Awe' (see page 83) which aren't really festivals but are every bit as important. But with the obsessive craving for knowledge you've probably developed, you must have known that already.

Revision Summary

There you go, then — that was the Judaism section. And what a section it was. Full of mitzvot, synagogues, covenants and rabbis, plus plenty more besides. Yep, this is the kind of stuff that you won't get very far without knowing (if you're doing one of the Judaism modules). So I'll tell you what I'd do if I were you. I'd learn all the stuff from the section, and then I'd try these questions. And if I got any wrong, I'd go back and have another look at the section, and then try the questions again. And I'd keep doing this until I could answer all the questions without making any mistakes. That seems like a good idea to me. And I'm sure you think the same, eh... So don't let me keep you — try the questions and see how you do...

1) Explain what part each of the following men played in the development of Judaism:
   a) Abraham, b) Moses, c) David.
2) What does the 'covenant' mean in Judaism?
3) Make a list of 11 things which the Jews believe about God.
4) Jews think of themselves as a 'chosen people'. What do they mean by this?
5) Describe what is meant by Zionism.
6) Why were some Jews unhappy about the establishment of the State of Israel in 1948?
7) Describe the following:
   a) Tenakh, b) Torah, c) Nevi'im, d) Ketuvim, e) Mishnah, f) Gemara, g) Talmud, h) Responsa.
8) Give 2 examples of occasions on which a Jewish person might consult a Bet Din.
9) What do Jews mean by 'Halakhah'?
10) What was the Holocaust?
11) What is meant by anti-Semitism?
12) What kind of theological questions have the Jews had to face as a result of the Holocaust? What alternative answers have they come up with?
13) What are a) Secular Jews, b) Hasidim, c) Progressive Jews?
14) Explain how and why Reform and Liberal Judaism began.
15) What do Jews mean by the word 'mitzvot'?
16) Explain the different attitudes towards mitzvot held by Orthodox and Progressive Jews.
17) What is a 'mikveh'? When might one be used?
18) Describe: a) Magen David, b) Menorah, c) Aron Hakodesh, d) Sefer Torah, e) Bimah, f) Ner Tamid.
19) What are the duties of a) a rabbi? b) a chazan?
20) Why are there no pictures of God in a Jewish home or synagogue?
21) What is a mezuzah?
22) Name and describe the 4 special Jewish prayer garments.
23) Explain what might happen at 'Brit Milah'. What is meant by 'redemption of the first-born'?
24) Describe how a Jewish boy might celebrate becoming 'Bar Mitzvah'.
25) Name 2 'coming of age' ceremonies for Jewish girls.
26) What is meant by Sheol?
27) Make a list of 8 Jewish mourning customs.
28) Why do Jews celebrate Shabbat?
29) Explain how a Jewish family celebrates Shabbat a) in the synagogue, b) in the home.
30) What is a pilgrimage?
31) Name 3 sites in the Holy Land which Jews especially like to visit. Explain why each is important.
32) What are 'kashrut'?
33) Why might a Jew fast?
34) List 8 major Jewish festivals (including the Days of Awe). Write down what each one commemorates.

Basic Islamic Beliefs

This stuff is the absolute fundamentals of Islam.
You won't get very far in your study of Islam if you don't know something about Tawhid and the Five Pillars.

Tawhid is the belief in the Oneness of God

1) Islam teaches that nothing is remotely like Allah, and nothing can be compared to him.
2) The worst sin for a Muslim would be to believe that God was not supreme — this concept is called Shirk. (Shirk is the opposite of tawhid.)

Allah is the Muslim name for God.

Muslim beliefs about Allah...
Allah is beyond time and space. He is the Almighty One, the Compassionate and the Merciful. All men and women owe their creation, and continued existence, to Allah — the One and Only Creator.

And see pages 7 and 9 for more basic Muslim beliefs about God.

The Five Pillars — a Guide to Islam

For Muslims, there is no point in having faith if you don't act on your beliefs.
And this action should be based on the Five Pillars — which are a kind of guide to Muslim life:

See pages 95 and 96 for more info about the Five Pillars of Islam.

1. **SHAHADAH — the Muslim Declaration of Faith**
   "*There is no god but Allah, and Muhammad is the Prophet of Allah.*" Muslims should repeat this several times a day.

2. **SALAH — Prayer five times a day**
   This is the second most important duty in Islam, and should be learnt from the age of 12. Exposed parts of the body, including feet and inside the mouth and nostrils, are washed three times before praying. If you happen to be waterless (e.g. in the desert) clean sand will do instead of water. This washing is called wudu.

3. **ZAKAH — Giving money or possessions to help the poor, sick and needy**
   It's compulsory in Islam, and the minimum is 2.5% of your disposable income. Each individual decides whether to give to a relative, to a charity, or to the poor — but come the Day of Judgement, you have to justify your decision.

4. **SAWM — Obligation to fast in Ramadan**
   Ramadan is the 9th month of the Muslim calendar, and celebrates Muhammad first receiving the revelation of the Qur'an. No food or drink can pass your lips during daylight hours — not even a cigarette or toothpaste are allowed. This fasting teaches self-discipline, which is believed to draw Muslims closer to Allah.

5. **HAJJ — Pilgrimage to Makkah at least once in your life** (if you're healthy and wealthy enough)
   This journey-of-a-lifetime is believed to teach equality — all men wear two unsewn cotton sheets, and women are covered from head to foot. So it doesn't matter how fat your wallet is — you're just like everyone else (like on the Day of Judgement).

Niyyah — it's the thought that counts...

In Islam, it's your intention (Niyyah) that's the key to how you're judged. If you fully intended doing something and you fail, it's counted as though you'd done it anyway. Unfortunately, this principle isn't carried over into your Exam, which seems a bit harsh really, if it's good enough for all other areas of life.

Prophets and Angels

According to the Qur'an, the prophets bring God's message so that people know how to behave. These prophets are not angels, they're humans — though they receive the message from an angel.

Risalah is the idea that Allah uses Messengers

1) Risalah is the concept of messengership, which is necessary in Islam because Allah is so great. He doesn't communicate directly with humans — instead he uses angels as messengers. Angels are created by Allah, require no food, drink or sleep, and obey Allah perfectly.
2) His mercy and compassion mean he cannot leave us to mess up our lives without doing something to help. So God gives messages to angels, who then pass on God's words to prophets (or rasuls).
3) In the Qur'an, the first man and the first prophet was Adam.
4) Allah sent many prophets as messengers, maybe because we seem to forget the plot quite quickly. The names of twenty-five prophets are mentioned in the Qur'an, although Muslim tradition suggests there have been 124,000.

Five Prophets are 'Mighty Ones'

1) Of all Allah's prophets, five are Mighty Ones. These are Nuh (Noah), Ibrahim (Abraham), Musa (Moses), Isa (Jesus) and Muhammad.
2) Ibrahim rejected the idea of many different gods, and it was Ibrahim who rebuilt the Ka'ba (the first structure built to worship one god) in Makkah. Ibrahim was also told by God to sacrifice his son as a test of his faith. After seeing that Ibrahim was prepared to do this, God told Ibrahim to kill a ram instead.
3) Moses is the only prophet that God spoke to directly rather than through the Angel Gabriel. He was given the tablets of the law (which Muslims believe is the foundation of all religion) on Mount Sinai. The Tawrat (Jews call it the Torah) is the Holy Book inspired by Moses.

According to Islam, the Zabur (a book like the Book of Psalms) was revealed to King David (see page 72 for more about David).

Allah said, "*O Jesus I am gathering you and causing you to ascend to Me, and am cleansing you of those who disbelieve, and am setting those who follow you above those who disbelieve.*" — Surah 3:55

The Injil (Gospel) was given to Isa (Jesus) according to Islam. It gives accounts of miracles, and explains the amazing life of Isa. But don't forget, Isa was just a prophet according to the Qur'an.

4) Allah sent Isa (Jesus) when he thought that humans had strayed from the teachings of Moses yet again. According to Islam, Isa was not crucified (God wouldn't allow it to happen) but after three years teaching he was taken up bodily into heaven to be with Allah.
5) Muhammad was the prophet to whom God revealed the Qur'an, in Arabic, for humanity to follow. Islam teaches that the Qur'an is the greatest miracle of all.

Khalifah — Taking Responsibility in God's name

1) Muslims believe in the idea of Judgement Day, when God will judge us on the basis of our actions. This suggests we have free will, and can choose how we act.
2) But Muslims also believe God has a divine master plan where everything is determined by him. In Islam this isn't a problem — we're not like God, and so we can't expect to understand all God's ways.

Al-Qadar is the Muslim idea of Allah's complete and final control over all events and destiny.

3) Khalifah is the idea that while we're on Earth we should take responsibility for the world in God's name, and make it the sort of place he wants it to be. However, if we fail to manage our task Allah will send help, which shows his compassion and mercy.

Muhammad is the Seal of the Prophets — but don't make my mistake...

This comes from the Qur'an — it means Muhammad's like the seal people used to attach to a letter to prove it had come from them, and to make sure nothing could be added. Muhammad was God's seal. But it does NOT mean that Muhammad balanced balls on his nose and made barking noises.

The Qur'an

Muslims believe the Qur'an is the most important book in the world, as it records the exact words of Allah (God). They call these words revelations, because they were revealed by Allah to the Prophet Muhammad.

The Qur'an is Treated with Respect

For Muslims, the Qur'an is...

1. **A COMPLETE RECORD OF ALLAH'S WORDS:** The Prophet never forgot any revelations, and his followers recorded them at once, and learned them by heart.
2. **A TOTALLY ACCURATE AND UNCHANGED RECORD** The early Caliph (Muslim ruler) Uthman made sure there was only one version and that it was completely correct.
3. **A COMPLETE GUIDE TO ISLAMIC LIFE** The Qur'an says what Muslims must believe, and how they must live, in order to get to Paradise. In the Qur'an, Allah tells Muslims what they need to know, so that they can please him. Since Muslims believe the Qur'an came direct from Allah, they trust it completely. Basically, if the Qur'an says 'Do this,' then a Muslim must do it.
4. **ALWAYS IN ARABIC** Allah gave the Qur'an to the Prophet Muhammad in Arabic. If you read it in another language, you might not get the proper meaning. So all Muslims must learn Arabic to be sure they are reading the real Qur'an.

Because the Qur'an is so important, Muslims treat it with great respect. Many Muslims will:

1) keep their Qur'an wrapped up to keep it clean,
2) wash their hands before touching it,
3) keep it on a higher shelf than all other books,
4) place it on a special stand when they read it.

The Qur'an is also read during private and public prayers, so Muslims get to know it really well. In the month of Ramadan, it's read from beginning to end during worship at the mosque.

The Qur'an is Divided into 114 Surahs

1) The Qur'an is organised into 114 surahs (chapters).
2) The surahs are arranged in order of length — longest first, shortest last (apart from Surah 1, the Fatihah, which is a short and punchy statement of central beliefs).
3) Each surah is made up of ayats (verses).
4) Most surahs begin with the bismillah — an Arabic phrase meaning 'In the name of Allah, the Merciful, the Compassionate'. This means that when Muslims start to read any Surah, they are reminded of the mercy and kindness of Allah.

The Hadith and the Sunnah are also Important Texts

Muslims also pay a lot of attention to the guidance and example they get from the following:

1. **THE HADITH** — the sayings of Muhammad which were not part of the Qur'an.
2. **THE SUNNAH** — the actions and way of life of Muhammad.

Because Muhammad was chosen by Allah to be his last Prophet, they regard him as a very remarkable man, and pay special attention to his words and actions.

Are you surah you've learnt all of this...

When Muslims read the Qur'an, they're learning about what Allah's like, how he relates to humans, and how to live the way Allah wants so they can get to Paradise and thus avoid the 'unpleasantness' of Hell. Basically, if it's in the Qur'an, it's important. And if it's important in Islam, it may well be in the Qur'an.

The Prophet Muhammad

A pretty central figure in Islam. If you're studying Islam, you'll want to know all this...

Muhammad's Early life was Hard

1) Muhammad was born around the year 570 AD/CE in Makkah (also known as Mecca). He had a hard childhood, after his parents died while he was young.
2) He married his widowed employer Khadijah at around the age of 25 — he had previously worked as her business manager.
3) The people of Makkah respected him, and called him Al-Amin — 'Mr Trustworthy'.

Life Changed in 610 CE — the call to be a Prophet

While he was meditating in a cave on Mount Nur, Allah sent the angel Jibrail (Gabriel) to him...

1) Jibrail passed on Allah's first command to Muhammad, "*Read, in the name of your Lord, who creates man out of a mere drop of blood.*" — Surah 96.

The letters 'pbuh' or 'pboh' are sometimes written after the name of Muhammad. They stand for 'Peace be upon (or on) Him'.

2) Although Muhammad was initially frightened, Khadijah helped him realise that God was calling him to be a prophet.
3) This was confirmed by the second command, "*Rise and Warn.*" — Surah 74. As time went on, Muhammad received loads more revelations from Allah.

This was the message that Muhammad had to take to the people of Makkah:

i) People were to worship one God, Allah — not many gods.
ii) People were to listen to him, because he was Allah's Prophet.
iii) People were to conduct their business honestly, and to look after the poor.
iv) If they did not do all this, they would burn in Hell.

4) Although a few people were converted, this was not a popular message. At first people laughed at him, or said he was mad. Then they started making life hard for his followers — even killing some. They also stopped Muhammad preaching within the city limits.
5) Finally, in 622, the Prophet and his followers had to leave Makkah. Muhammad was invited to become the leader of a place called Yathrib, which was eventually named after him — Madinah (or Medina) short for Medina Nabi, 'City of the Prophet'. Things got better for the Muslims in Madinah.
6) The journey to Madinah is called the Hijrah or the Emigration. It was a real turning point. Now, in the safety of Madinah, the Muslims could make many more converts, build a Muslim community, and develop their own way of life.
7) Many people see this as the real start of Islam — even the Muslim calendar starts from the Hijrah in 622.

Madinah and Makkah went to War

After the Hijrah, Madinah and Makkah were at war. The key events are these...

1) 624 — Battle of Badr. Muhammad won and became very popular in Madinah.
2) 625 — Battle of Uhud. Close, but Muhammad came out ahead on points.
3) 627 — Battle of the Trench. A brilliant victory for Muhammad, leading to...
4) 628 — Treaty of Hudaybiya – preparing the way for a Muslim takeover of Makkah in 630.
5) By Muhammad's death in 632, Makkah was a Muslim city and Islam was advancing through Arabia.

Mecca — they're magic for bingo...

Make sure you can explain why the Hijrah was so important. Madinah was good for Muhammad's followers — they'd got away from the hard times of Makkah, and they built up a Muslim way of life under the Prophet's leadership. Even now Muslims try to live the kind of life that the Muslim community did in Madinah.

Different Islamic Traditions

In Madinah, Muhammad and his followers formed a single community. But this didn't last. After he died, Muslims disagreed about who should be the next leader. This eventually led to a split.

Sunnis and Shi'ites Split after the Death of Ali

1) The next four leaders after Muhammad were chosen because they were good Muslims and competent leaders. These successors (or 'caliphs') were:

i) Abu Bakr: 632-634 CE ii) Umar: 634-644 CE iii) Uthman: 644-656 CE iv) Ali: 656-661 CE

2) However, some Muslims had wanted Muhammad's close relative Ali to be the first leader after Muhammad's death. Others said Ali should never be leader at all.
3) After Ali's death, two groups were formed — the Sunnis and the Shi'ites. Each group followed a different succession of leaders.
4) The Sunni accepted the next caliph (successor), but the Shi'ites (Shi'at Ali or Party of Ali) followed Ali's descendants.
5) Sunnis call the first four leaders after Muhammad the 'Rightly Guided Caliphs'. Shi'ites, on the other hand, believe the first three caliphs shouldn't have been leaders at all.
6) Sunnis and Shi'ites have been separate groups ever since the split, and often in conflict.

The Majority of Muslims are Sunnis

About 90% of Muslims are Sunni (or orthodox) Muslims. They believe:

1) The Rightly Guided Caliphs (including Ali) were properly chosen.
2) The followers of Ali were wrong to break away from the majority.
3) No one after Muhammad gets special knowledge from God (including imams).
4) Muslims should be guided by the consensus (majority view) of the community. In particular, it's the community that elects the caliphs. This is how the Rightly Guided Caliphs were chosen.
5) Paying special attention to Ali and his sons takes attention away from Allah and his Prophet (Muhammad), and is wrong.
6) The Qur'an is complete and unaltered, just as Allah revealed it to Muhammad.

In Sunni mosques, imam is simply a title of respect given to the mosque prayer leader. This is very different to Shi'ite beliefs.

Shi'ite Muslims have some Different Beliefs

Shi'ite Muslims are also referred to as Shi'i or Shi'a Muslims. They believe:

1) Ali was the first true leader after Muhammad, and all other leaders of Islam should be descendants of Muhammad.
2) Ali had special knowledge given by God to make sure his teaching and actions were right. After him, other leaders called imams had this knowledge too.
3) The last imam (most say the 12th, but some the 7th) went into hiding, and since then other leaders have been chosen by him. The most important of these are called ayatollahs (signs of Allah).
4) They take guidance from the Hadith (sayings) of Ali, as well as those of Muhammad.
5) They commemorate the martyrdom of Ali and his sons Hasan and Husayn — they have festivals concerned with Ali and his sons, and make pilgrimage to places connected with them.
6) Some Shi'ites believe that the Qur'an was altered by the Sunnis, so that verses which would back up the Shi'ites were got rid of.

An important group of Shi'ites believe that the 12th and last imam is still in hiding, but will eventually return to revitalise the Muslim community.

The Festival of Ashura

The most important festival is Ashura, celebrated on the 10th day of the month of Muharram at Karbala, where Husayn was killed. Shi'ites perform rituals re-enacting the event, and some even wound themselves to share in his suffering.

I Ashura you that this is important — so learn it...

Don't forget that although Sunnis and Shi'ites disagree over leadership and authority, they agree about a lot of important stuff — like Allah, Muhammad, the judgement, and the idea of Shari'ah, so they have a lot in common. Don't forget that, or you may find that your shoes turn into some kind of thick gooey cheese.

Sufism

For Sufis (as for all Muslims) the Qur'an is the fundamental guide in matters relating to their religious faith. What makes Sufis different from other Muslims is the way they interpret this guide.

Sufism is a Mystical Movement

1) Sufism is often called Islamic mysticism — the aim is to be at one with God and reach truths beyond human understanding. It developed as a reaction to the growing attachment to a life of making money.

2) For Sufis, a symbolic or mystical meaning lies beneath the actual words of the Qur'an. To find this meaning, it's necessary to purify your thoughts and actions, and be constantly aware of the love of God in order to achieve a 'joining together' with Allah.

3) Sufis believe that the Prophet Muhammad is the man who most perfectly achieved this close relationship with God — so they try to imitate his way of life. They live a humble life — based on asceticism (self-denial) and meditation, and make use of ritual practices, like sacred dances or chanting.

4) Sufis have tried to show that the heart of Islam is not how a Muslim practises their faith, but the bond between each person and God. In other words Sufis encourage Muslims to look at their relationship with God, instead of just obeying the rules.

"It is not enough to observe the rituals of Islam... A humble soul may be religious even though ignorant of interpretations of the Qur'an. The core of religion is to repent of one's sins, purge the heart of all but God."
— 12th century Sufi philosopher Al-Ghazzali.

Jalaluddin Rumi (a 13th century Sufi master) founded a group which uses music and dance to spin at speed. The spinning of these 'Whirling Dervishes' is said to lead to a trancelike state, and is regarded as a form of prayer.

Women have played a big part in Sufism

1) Women have played a big part in Sufism from its beginnings. Fatima (the daughter of Muhammad and his wife Khadijah) is often regarded as the first Muslim mystic.

2) And as the mystical side of Islam developed, it was a woman, Rabi'a al-Adawiyya, who first described God as the "Beloved". She also gave meaning to the idea that ultimately it is through love that people are brought into unity with God.

Sufism is Different to other Islamic Traditions

Sufism's ideas about the relationship between people and God are different from other Islamic traditions.

1) Islam is based on the idea of duty — the word Muslim even means 'one who surrenders his or her life to Allah'. Muslims must follow the Five Pillars and the teaching of the Qur'an.

2) Muslims generally emphasise the radical difference between God and human beings.

3) The idea promoted by some Sufi groups of merging with God would not be acceptable to many Muslims.

How's it going? — Sufi, so good...

Religion is like any other 'people' thing — people are different, and will want different things from their religion. But that's no bad thing, I say — variety is the spice of life. As a friend of mine once said, "If we were all swimming the same way, we'd never meet anyone coming in the other direction." I think.

Islam and the Shari'ah

'Islam' literally means 'submission' or 'obedience' to Allah. And there are certain day-to-day rules that Allah expects you to follow if you want to show that you're being obedient.

Being Obedient to Allah is Vital for a Muslim

Yep. Muslims should be obedient. The reasoning is as follows...

1) Allah expects obedience, and obedience is a Muslim's duty.
2) If a Muslim does his or her duty, that person will please Allah.
3) If a person pleases Allah enough, they will be sent to Paradise after they die.
4) And if Allah is not pleased with someone, they will be punished after they die.

So this is vital stuff. How a Muslim lives in this life will determine where he or she ends up in the next life.

The Shari'ah Contains the Rules for Islamic Life

Fortunately, Allah makes sure Muslims know what to do and how to live.

1) The first and most important source of guidance for a Muslim is the Qur'an. But this doesn't give every detail, and it doesn't talk about 21st-century issues — like drugs, for example.
2) So Muslims need extra day-to-day guidance and this is found in the law-code called the shari'ah.

'Shari'ah' means 'straight path' in Arabic — and it keeps Muslims 'going straight'. If Muslims obey Shari'ah, they can be sure they're doing what Allah wants.

The Shari'ah is Based on the Qur'an

Scholars and lawyers built up much of the shari'ah from these three sources in the early years of Islam. They're the most important sources of Islamic law.

1. **THE QUR'AN** — The shari'ah is based on the Qur'an. Any moral guidance in the Qur'an is bound to be in the shari'ah.
2. **THE HADITH AND SUNNAH** — The shari'ah also takes guidance from the Hadith (sayings) and Sunnah (lifestyle) of Muhammad.
3. **MUSLIM CUSTOM AND PRACTICE** — It then looks to the custom and practice of the Muslim community, especially if it can be traced back to the time when Muhammad was alive.

But if the first three don't help with some new problem, the scholars will appeal to two more:

4. **CONSENSUS OR AGREEMENT** — Based on their knowledge of the Qur'an and of Islamic tradition, the most learned scholars would reach an agreement about how to act. They trust Allah to make sure they get it right.
5. **ANALOGY OR SIMILARITY** — If they can't find guidance on any particular issue, they look for guidance on something similar. The Qur'an says nothing about heroin, for example, but it does forbid alcohol. Both are bad for the user, so the scholars can work out that if alcohol is out, then so are other drugs.

Drawing on all these, the shari'ah covers the whole of a Muslim's life.

Don't get caught by the long arm of the shari'ah...

So that's pretty much where Islamic law comes from then. And it's pretty important too. Well, it certainly is if you're a Muslim, anyway. And it certainly is if you're studying Islam and you've got an Exam coming up. So although I'm not actually God, I command you to learn all the above. For your own sake, of course.

Islamic Living and Jihad

You need to know about some particular bits of the shari'ah laws which affect a Muslim's daily life.

The Shari'ah says things are either Halal or Haram

HALAL means 'allowed' **HARAM means 'forbidden'**

You need to know these two Arabic words. Think of the letter L — haLaL is aLLowed. And HARaM can HARM.

Dress Laws — Basic Principles are Modesty and Cleanliness

1) Everyone should wear loose, modest clothing, so they don't arouse desire. (Sexy figure-hugging clothes are definitely out.)
2) Outside the home, women should wear the hijab (a veil which covers the hair) so that nothing is visible but the face, hands and feet.
3) Men should not wear flashy clothing — e.g. no silk or gold jewellery.

Some Muslims say this is out of date, especially in western countries, but others stick to it because it was the custom of Muhammad's own wives.

Food Laws — No Pork, No Blood at all, No animals that Eat Meat

1) The basic rules are no pork, no blood at all, and no animals that eat meat.
2) This means it's very important how an animal is killed — it must be done by slitting the neck and allowing all the blood to drain out. Meat from animals killed like this is halal, i.e. allowed.
3) Food preparation is also important — no animal fat can be used (but vegetable oil is okay).
4) Fish and vegetables are fine, but they must be cooked without animal fat.

Alcohol and Gambling are Definitely Out

Alcohol is definitely not allowed (see page 41), and neither is gambling. This is due to the damage they can cause to yourself and others — and it's a basic principle of shari'ah that a Muslim should not harm others.

i) The thinking is that people do stupid things when they're drunk, and don't think about obeying Allah. They also hurt others with behaviour like drink-driving.
ii) And if you win money by gambling, it is only because someone else has lost it.

No Charging Interest on Loans

Charging high rates of interest on loans is called usury — in Arabic this is called riba.

Shari'ah also forbids any financial deals involving interest. This is to prevent rich people making more money at the expense of poorer people, and to make sure wealth is spread more fairly. This means Muslims can't use most Western bank accounts. Also, Muslim businesses must be run differently from others, because the Western economic system depends on lending money and charging interest. So Muslims really need a separate banking system.

There are Two Kinds of Jihad

Jihad in Arabic means 'striving', and is often misunderstood by non-Muslims.
Most Muslims believe there are two kinds of Jihad.

THE GREATER JIHAD

This is every Muslim's personal struggle to obey Allah, follow Shari'ah and become a better Muslim. It's a tough spiritual struggle, lasts a lifetime, and affects every aspect of life. But winning this struggle gets you to Paradise.

THE LESSER JIHAD

This is the struggle to make the world a better place. Part of this means struggling against evils like poverty and injustice, and part of it is the struggle to defend Islam against its enemies. However, both the Qur'an and the shari'ah teach that this should only be in self-defence. There's a big debate over where terrorism fits in, but most Muslims stick with the simple rule that killing is wrong (haram) except in personal self-defence.

See also page 40.

Examic jihad — striving for good exam grades...

Hmmm... somehow it seems difficult to see Mick Jagger fitting into the Muslim lifestyle, I reckon. But it probably doesn't matter — I haven't heard that he wants to turn to Islam. So... learn the four subheadings above about shari'ah law, and the stuff about the two kinds of jihad, and you'll be laughing come Exam time.

The Mosque

A mosque (or masjid) is more than a place of worship — it's also a centre of the community for Muslims. Masjid literally means 'place of prostration' (i.e. lying with the face down) — an act of submission to God.

A Mosque (Masjid) is the Muslim House of Prayer

1) The Prophet Muhammad said that any clean place could be used for worship.
2) Some mosques are extremely simple, others are very grand, but all have a dome representing the universe.
3) All mosques will have at least one minaret. This is a tall tower from where the muezzin (mu'adhin in Arabic) calls the adhan (call to prayer).

Inside the Mosque

1) Beautiful coloured mosaic tiles, or richly coloured Arabic calligraphy (writing) often decorate both the outside and inside of a mosque.
2) Shoes must be left at the door, and every mosque must have somewhere for Muslims to wash before prayer.
3) There are no pictures of Muhammad or Allah, since no one is allowed to draw them.
4) There are no seats, but the whole floor is usually covered with rich carpet.
5) There is little in the way of furniture, but you will see a pulpit (called a minbar), where the imam (a respected person) will lead prayers from — especially on Fridays.
6) Muslims face Makkah when they pray, and a special niche (called the mihrab) in the 'direction-wall' shows the direction in which Makkah lies.

Apart from prayer, a mosque is used as a Madrassah (a Mosque school), where Muslims learn the general principles of Islam, as well as how to carry out Muslim practices and recite the Qur'an.

MEN, WOMEN AND THE MOSQUE

The main service in the Mosque is on Friday, and all males are expected to attend unless they're ill or travelling.

Women don't have to attend the mosque, but if they do they must pray separately from men. Also, women do not lead prayers in a mosque if a man is available, but they may lead other women and children.

Sunni Imams are Different from Shi'ite Imams

1) In the Sunni Muslim tradition (about 90% of all Muslims are Sunni), the imam is sometimes a paid member of the community. However, any person who has a good knowledge of Islam and is of good character can act as imam, and anyone who knows the prayer can lead it.
2) The imam teaches about the Qur'an, and leads the prayers, but he is not a 'holy man'. He may also visit the sick, and care for those who have had a death in the family.
3) In the minority Shi'ite Muslim tradition, the imam is different — he is a successor of Muhammad, and is considered semi-divine.

Sunni and Shi'ite — Didn't they sing 'I got you, babe'...

The mosque is central to an Islamic community — and is much more than just a place to go and pray. This business of praying in the direction of Makkah is also taken seriously — some Muslims carry a special compass to enable them to pray in the right direction, even when they're nowhere near a mosque.

Worship and Prayer

To a Muslim all life is worship. Every part of life is lived in a way that will please Allah and show obedience to him. If it's done with Allah in mind, then it's worship. It all comes down to the Five Pillars of Islam.

Muslim Worship is all about the Five Pillars

Shahadah — the First Pillar of Islam

'There is no God but Allah, and Muhammad is the Prophet of Allah.'

This leads to obligations — if Allah's the only God, then Muslims should pray to Allah, and only to Allah.

Salah (Prayer) — the Second Pillar

You can't be a Muslim without praying in the way Muhammad did. Regular prayer keeps Allah in a Muslim's mind. It also keeps Muslims aware of their duty to obey Allah.

1) Muslims should pray five times a day — at sunrise, early afternoon, late afternoon, after sunset, and late at night.
2) The muezzin makes the call to prayer (adhan) from the minaret of a mosque. (The words of the call to prayer are on page 97.)
3) Ideally prayer should take place in a mosque. If this isn't possible, a prayer mat should be used to make a prayer place.
4) Wudu (washing before prayer) is important (see page 86). This is because a Muslim must be pure and clean when approaching Allah.
5) A Muslim should face Makkah (Muhammad's place of birth) when praying. The direction of Makkah is called the qiblah. A compass can be used to find the qiblah (which in England is roughly southeast).
6) There is a set ritual for prayer — this is known as the rak'ah (and the rak'ah may be repeated several times at each prayer session). Each rak'ah involves standing, then kneeling, then putting your forehead to the ground as a sign of submission.
7) If several Muslims are praying in one place, then they all do the ritual together as a sign of unity.
8) Friday prayers are called Salat-al-Jum'ah (or just Jum'ah) — it's a community occasion, and at least 40 people should be there, all praying together.

Women and men pray separately — so people keep their mind on Allah rather than on the opposite sex.

Salah is compulsory prayer. Extra prayers are called Du'a, and Muslims can do these at any time. In Du'a prayers, beads can be used — 99 beads for the 99 names of Allah.

Benefits of Prayer

1) Keeps you in close contact with Allah and stops you forgetting him.
2) Expression of solidarity — doing exactly the same as all other Muslims.
3) Moral and spiritual discipline.

Problems with Praying in 'non-Muslim' countries

In non-Muslim countries it can often be hard to pray at the right time, e.g. when you have to go to school or work. This is one of the ways in which life is more complicated for Muslims if they live in a country where Islam is not the way of life of most people.

Zakah — the Third Pillar

This is another practical way of showing obedience — it's a way of redistributing wealth to poorer Muslims.

1) Wealth is given by Allah, so it should be used to serve Allah.
2) The amount donated is usually 2½% of a person's income. It's given to the mosque and is then redistributed to needy Muslims, or used for religious purposes like Muslim schools.
3) It's a sign of concern for others and encourages unselfishness.
4) A Muslim must pay zakah, but giving extra charity is also okay (see page 35).

Makkah, Zakah and Rak'ah — this page is a cracker... boom boom...

As with many things in Muslim life, the Five Pillars have their basis in the Qur'an and the life of Muhammad. The shahadah is taken from the Qur'an, while the salah was required of Muhammad (and later his followers). And as for the zakah, well, that's supposed to reflect Muhammad's generosity during his lifetime.

Worship and Prayer

The last two pillars of Islam are to do with fasting and pilgrimage.

Sawm — the Fourth Pillar

1) Muslims must fast between sunrise and sunset during the month of Ramadan in the Muslim calendar.
2) This fasting means no food, no drink, no smoking and no sex.
3) Also, there must be no angry words, no swearing, no gossiping, no lying and no bad behaviour.
4) Ramadan is a time of both physical and moral self-discipline, and a time of total obedience to Allah.
5) It's supposed to help Muslims understand hunger, and so makes them more willing to help others.
6) It's also a time to show publicly that Allah matters more than any physical needs.

There are exceptions to the normal Ramadan rules:
1) Children don't have to fast until they're about 12 years old.
2) People can be excused for medical reasons. Those who are ill (and women having their period) are excused. And it's okay to take medicine which has to be regular, e.g. antibiotics.
3) If you're on a journey, you can be excused. But you have to make up the missed days later.

Thanksgiving for the Qur'an

Ramadan is also the month Muhammad received the first revelation of the Qur'an. So the Ramadan fast is also a period of thanksgiving for the Qur'an, and over the month of Ramadan it's read from beginning to end during prayers at the mosque.

Id-ul-Fitr

Id-ul-Fitr is a joyful day marking the end of Ramadan. Muslims attend the mosque for special prayers to thank Allah for the benefits of Ramadan, and often exchange cards and have family parties. However, the important thing is the fast, not the end of it.

Hajj (Pilgrimage to Makkah) — the Fifth Pillar

1) Muslims must make the pilgrimage once in their lifetime, as long as they can afford it and they are strong enough to cope with it.
2) Hajj is a visit to where Muhammad lived and preached, following in his footsteps and in those of the prophets Adam, Ibrahim, and Ismail. It makes stories of the prophets 'come alive' for Muslims.
3) Special pilgrim clothing called ihram is worn by all pilgrims, rich and poor. This clothing is very basic, and shows equality before Allah.
4) Once at Makkah, Muslims must do seven circuits of the Ka'ba, touching the stone if possible — this ritual is called the tawaf.
5) Next, a pilgrim must make seven journeys between the hills of Safa and Marwa (where Hagar searched for water for her son Ismail). This part of the pilgrimage is called the Sa'y. Pilgrims then draw water from the Zamzam Well, which Allah made for Hagar.
6) The next stage is a journey to Mount Arafat, where pilgrims stand and pray for Allah's forgiveness. This is where Muslims believe Adam was forgiven after being thrown out of Eden, and also where the Last Judgement will take place.
7) Stones are then thrown at three pillars in Mina, to symbolise driving the Devil away.
8) Near the end comes Id-ul-Adha — a 4-day festival. This consists of prayer at the mosque, then a family gathering, which includes a sacrifice of sheep, goat or chicken, shared with the poor.
9) The title 'Hajji' is given to those who complete this pilgrimage.

Muslims believe the Ka'ba was built by Adam, rebuilt by Ibrahim, and purified by Muhammad. It's a giant stone cube, covered with black cloth, and is said to be the first man-made structure dedicated to a single God.

The Last Judgement — yeah, when is the Exam exactly...

Yep, the Five Pillars of Islam are an incredibly important part of a Muslim's life, but I reckon you must have guessed that by now. If you're studying Islam, then you won't be wanting to go into the Exam without knowing quite a lot about all five pillars. Unless you have some kind of 'Exam death wish', that is.

Birth and Death Ceremonies

Every child is born with a 'clean slate', with the chance of becoming a good Muslim, pleasing Allah and reaching Paradise. After death comes judgement, followed by reward or punishment.

'Allah' should be the First Word a Child Hears

The first word a child should hear is the name of Allah. As soon as it is born the call to prayer (adhan) is whispered in its ear.

The adhan begins '*Allahu Akbar...*' (God is the Greatest...).

It continues, '*I bear witness there is no God but Allah, I bear witness that Muhammad is the Messenger of Allah, Rush to Prayer, Rush to Success, God is the Greatest...*'

So the first words a child hears are the most central teachings of Islam.

See also page 13 for more on Muslim beliefs about death.

Aqiqa — The Naming Ceremony

1) At seven days old the child's head is shaved, and a donation given to the poor of gold or silver weighing at least as much as the hair. This brings Allah's blessing on the child.
2) It's traditional to make a sacrifice to Allah as a sign of thanksgiving. One sheep or goat for a girl — two for a boy. The meat is shared among the family, after 1/3 of it has been given away to the hungry.

3) The child is then named — there are two traditional kinds of name:
   a) it could be named after one of the Prophet's family or companions,
   b) it could be given a name which shows obedience to Allah.
4) This ceremony generally involves a party and a lot of celebration.
5) For boys, circumcision (removal of the foreskin) is also required. Often it's done in hospital soon after birth, but in some countries it's a separate ceremony at 7 or 8 years old.

For example, Abdullah (servant of Allah) or Abd-ur-Rahman (servant of the Merciful One).

'Allah' should be the Last Word a Person Hears

A Muslim hopes not to die alone, but with relatives and friends around, who will:

i) Keep them company and look after them.
ii) Ensure last-minute business is settled, so the dying one is not distracted by things to do with this life.
iii) Pray, and recite '*There is no God but Allah,*' so that the person may be helped to concentrate on the name of God. Ideally, just as the name of Allah was the first thing the Muslim heard at birth, it should also be the last at death.

Bodies are Buried Facing Makkah

1) After a person has died, the body is washed, as a sign of respect.
2) The body is then wrapped in a clean white shroud.
3) Funeral prayers (Janazah prayers) are said, praying that the dead person may be judged mercifully and gain a place in Paradise.
4) The body is buried in a simple grave, lying on its right side with the face towards Makkah.
5) A period of mourning is kept for three days, finishing with Qur'an reading and prayers for the dead person. Some Muslims do this after 40 days as well.

It's said that graves are visited by two angels to question the deceased and work out whether they're fit for the next life.

Judgement, then reward or punishment — sounds like Exams...

Islam is a 'total life' thing — with 'Allah' being the first and last word that a person hears. Muhammad's actions at the death of his son are even taken as a guide to the right way to behave at the death of a loved one — Muhammad cried, meaning that Muslims aren't ashamed to cry at the death of a friend or relative.

Revision Summary

That's it — that's the end of the book. Well, almost. There's still the little matter of these revision questions. They test all the things you'll need to know about if you're going to do well in the Islam part of your Exam. So try them, and see how you do. Then if you get any wrong, revise the stuff that was causing problems and have another go. And keep doing this until none of it causes any problems at all.
Well, what are you waiting for... stop shirking and get on with it.

1) Explain what 'tawhid' means to a Muslim. What is 'shirk'?
2) Name the Five Pillars of Islam.
3) What is niyyah?
4) Who delivers God's messages to the prophets? What is the Arabic word for this idea of messengership?
5) How many prophets are mentioned in the Qur'an? Who was the first prophet?
6) What are the names of the five Mighty Prophets? What's the Arabic word for this kind of prophet?
7) What's the (Islamic) name of the holy book inspired by Moses?
8) Explain what is meant by 'Khalifah'.
9) In what way was Muhammad the 'Seal of the Prophets'?
10) Explain why the Qur'an is so important for Muslims.
11) What is a surah? And an ayat?
12) What phrase does each surah of the Qur'an begin with?
13) What is the Hadith? And the Sunnah?
14) Describe the 4 main teachings that Muhammad was to preach to the people of Makkah.
15) Describe the initial reaction to Muhammad in Makkah after he started preaching the teachings of Allah.
16) Explain what the Hijrah was. Where did it end?
17) Name 4 important battles fought between Madinah and Makkah.
18) Why did Sunni and Shi'ite Muslims became two separate groups within Islam? Describe the differences between the beliefs of the two groups.
19) Explain how the Qur'an is interpreted by Sufis.
20) What is a Whirling Dervish?
21) Explain why it's important for a Muslim to be obedient to Allah?
22) Name the 3 main sources of shari'ah law. What happens if no guidance on a particular issue can be found in these sources?
23) What do the following terms mean: a) halal, b) haram?
24) Describe 4 things in shari'ah law that are of day-to-day importance for a Muslim.
25) Describe the 2 different kinds of jihad.
26) What is the Arabic word for mosque?
27) Describe what you'd see if you went into a typical mosque.
28) Describe the role of an imam in the Sunni tradition.
29) Explain the following terms: a) muezzin, b) adhan, c) wudu, d) qiblah, e) rak'ah, f) du'a.
30) What is the Third Pillar of Islam?
31) Explain what Muslims must do during the month of Ramadan, as required by the Fourth Pillar of Islam.
32) What is Id-ul-Fitr?
33) Explain what is meant by 'Hajj' in Islam. Describe the customs and festivals associated with Hajj.
34) What is meant by 'aqiqa'? Describe some of the Islamic rituals concerned with the birth of a baby.
35) Describe some of the Islamic rituals connected with death.

Index

A
abortion 14, 16, 17, 48
Abraham 72
absolute morality 50
Adam 8, 87
adhan 95, 97
Adolf Hitler 75
Adonai 73
adultery 18, 21, 22
Advent 61
afterlife 11, 12
agape 47
Akhirah 13
Albert Einstein 3
alcohol 41, 93
Ali 90
Allah 7, 13, 86, 88, 89, 94
Al-Qadar 13
Alpha Courses 51
altar 57, 58
Amnesty International 28
angel 87
Anglican Church 53, 55
animals 37
annulment 21
anti-Semitism 75
apartheid 27
apologetics 50
Apostles' Creed 45
Apostolic Succession 54
aqiqa 97
Arafat 96
Archbishop of Canterbury 55
architecture 58
Ark 78
artificial insemination 18
Ascension 45, 61
Ash Wednesday 61
Ashkenazi Jews 76
Ashura 90
assisted suicide 15
Assumption 54, 61
ayatollah 90

B
baptism 57, 62, 63, 65
Baptists 53, 57, 58
Bar Mitzvah 80
Barabbas 70
Bat Chayil 80
Bat Mitzvah 80
Beatitudes 49
Bet Din 22, 74
Bet Haknesset 78
Bible 2, 26, 46
Big Bang 3, 10
bimah 78
birth control 14
bishop 55
Bismillah 88
blasphemy 43, 65, 67, 70
Body of Christ 52
Book of Job 9
Brandt Report 34
Brit Milah 80
Buffy 64
bullying 48

C
CAFOD 34, 36
caliph 90
Canaan 72
cannabis 41
cantor (see chazan)
capel 79
capital punishment 38
cardinal 55
Catechism 54
cathedral 55, 58
celibacy 20, 24
challot 82
chapel 56
charismatic worship 54, 60
charity 34, 35
Charles Darwin 10
chastity 51
chazan 78, 82
cheesecake 84
chosen people 29, 73
Christ 45, 65
christening 57
Christian Aid 34, 36
Christmas 61
Christmas pudding 62
Church of England 53, 55
ciborium 60
circumcision 72, 97
Cliff Richard 12
Codes 74
coffee mornings 57
cohabit 20
Communion of Saints 11, 52
community service 38
compassion 14, 15, 34
concentration camp 75
confirmation 57, 62, 63
conflict 68
conscience 2, 48
conscientious objectors 39
conservative view 46
contemplation 62
contraception 14, 16, 17
corporal punishment 38
cosmological theories 10
counselling 64
covenant 72
creation 10
creed 60
crime 38
crown of thorns 70
crucifixion 45, 61, 70
crusades 31, 39

D
dachshund 66
David 72
Day of Judgement
9, 13, 17, 36, 38, 87
Days of Awe 83
deacon 55
death penalty 38
decalogue 47
denomination 53, 54
design arguments 3
Desmond Tutu 28
developing nations 36
Devil 6, 7, 8, 41
diaspora 73
Dietrich Bonhoeffer 28
diocese 55
disarmament 39
discipleship 69
discrimination 26, 28, 32, 39
divorce 21, 22, 23
dogma 54
double effect 15
doughnut 84
dowry 23
dreaded skin disease 67
drugs 41

E
Easter 61
Easter bunnies 61
ecumenism 52
egg donation 18
environment 36
Epiphany 61
equality 26, 29, 30
eros 47
Eucharist (see Holy Communion)
euthanasia 15, 16, 17
evangelism 51, 54
Evensong 57
evidence 2
evil 8, 9, 75
evolution 10
EXIT 15
exodus 84
experiments 2
extended family 21
extraordinary treatment 15
extreme unction 62
eye of a needle 66

F
faith 2, 68
fasting 62, 83, 86, 96
fertiliser 18
fertility treatment 18
figure-hugging clothes 93
Final Solution 75
first communion 63
Five Pillars of Islam 7, 86, 91, 95, 96
foetus 14
font 57, 63
forgiveness 48
Free Churches 53, 58
fundamentalism 46
funeral 57, 64

G
gambling 34, 35, 93
Gemara 74
Gemilut Hasadim 35
general revelation 4
Gethsemene 70
global warming 36
goat 66, 97
God slot 42
godparents 63
Golgotha 70
Good Friday 61
Good Samaritan 26
Great Schism 53
Greenhouse Effect 36
grief 64, 81
groovy 56

H
Hadith 88, 92
Hajj 7, 30, 86, 96
Halakhah 74
halal 93
Hanukkah 84
haram 93
Hashem 73
Hasidic Jews 76
Heaven 11, 12
Hell 11, 12, 13
Hijab 30
Hijrah 89
historical truth 2
Holocaust 75
Holy Communion
41, 46, 54, 58, 60, 62
Holy Land 31, 56, 62
holy matrimony 20, 62
Holy Spirit 5, 6, 15, 45
holy war 39, 40
Holy Week 61
homily 60
homosexuality 24
hospice 15
hot-cross bun 62
hotch-potch of other stuff 74
House Churches 53
House of Life 12
huppah 22
hymn 58, 60
hypocrisy 49, 50

I
I got you, babe 94
Iblis 7
icon 32, 58, 62
Id-ul-Adha 96
Id-ul-Fitr 96
ihram 96
Imam 90, 94
immaculate conception 54
immanent 5, 6, 7
impersonal god 5
incarnation 45
Internet 43
Issac Newton 3

J
Jahannam 13
Jerusalem 72, 73
Jihad 40, 93
Jimi Hendrix 41
John the Baptist 63
Jonah 29
Judas 70
judiciary 38
just war 31, 39
justice 48

K
Ka'ba 96
kaddish 81
kashrut 83
ketubah 22
ketuvim 74
khalifah 37, 87
kiddush 82
kiddushin 22
kippah 79
kosher 74, 83

L
laity 55
L'Arche 51
Last Supper 60, 66, 70
Law of Moses 47, 49
lay ministry 52
lectern 57
Lent 61
Liberal Judaism 12, 76
liberal view 46
Liberation Theology 54
life after death 11, 12, 13, 45
life-support machine 11, 16
literalism 46
liturgy 57, 60
Liturgy of the Word 60
Lots 84
love 47

Index

lych-gate 56

M

magen David 78
magisterium 46, 54
mahr 23
Makkah 86, 87, 89, 94, 95, 97
Mardi Gras 61
marriage 20, 22, 23, 24, 62, 69
Martin Luther King 28, 49
martyr 39, 40
Mary Magdalene 70
Masada 83
masjid 94
Masorti movement 76
mass (see Holy Communion)
Maundy Thursday 61
meaning of life 1
Mecca (see Makkah)
media 27, 42, 43
meditation 62
menorah 78
mercy killing 15
Messiah 12, 45, 65, 72
Messianic secret 69
Methodists 53, 57, 60
mezuzah 79
midnight mass 61
mihrab 94
mikveh 77, 78, 81
milchemet mitzvah 40
milchemet reshut 40
minbar 94
mind-boggling stuff 7
minimum wage 34
minyan 29
miracle 3, 7, 67, 68
mishnah 74
missionary 31
mitzvot 38, 74, 77
monotheism 5, 73
moral evil 8
moral truth 2
Moses 72, 84, 87
mosque 31, 88, 94, 95
Mother Teresa 49
Mount Sinai 72, 87
mu'adhin 94, 95
muezzin (see mu'adhin)
Muhammad
30, 86, 87, 88, 89, 90, 91, 92, 94, 95, 96
music 1, 58

N

National Lottery 34
nationalism 30
natural evil 8
natural law 14
nave 57
near-death experiences 11
Ner Tamid 78
Nevi'im 74
New Testament 46
Nicene Creed 6
nikah 23
niyyah 86
Noahide Code 32, 37
nonconformists 53
nuclear family 21
nuclear war 39
numinous 3, 4

O

Old Testament 46, 74
omnipotent 6
omnipresent 5, 6
omniscient 6, 53
ordained ministry 52, 55
ordination 55, 62
original sin 63
Orthodox Church 53, 58
Orthodox Jews 12, 76, 77
Oscar Romero 28

P

pacifism 39, 40
pagan 56
Palm Sunday 61
parables 66
paranormal 11
Passover 70, 84
patriarch 55
Penitential Rite 60
Pentecost 61
persecution 75
personal god 5
Pesach 80, 84
Peter 70
Pharisees 67, 68, 69
philia 47
Philistines 72
phylacteries 79
Pilate 70
pilgrimage 30, 62, 83, 86, 90, 96
pluralism 31
polygamy 24
polytheism 5
pope 52, 53, 54, 55
population growth 34
pork 93
pornography 43
poverty 34, 35, 51
prayer 62, 82, 86, 95
prejudice 26, 27, 28, 31, 32
Presbyterian Church 55
prisoners of conscience 28, 39
pro-choice argument 14
Progressive Jews 76, 77, 80
promiscuity 24
proof 2
prophets 7, 74, 87
proportionality 39
Protestant 53
pulpit 57
punishment 38, 48
Purgatory 11
Purim 80, 84

Q

qiblah 95
Quakers 14, 37, 53, 63
Qur'an 30, 86, 88, 91, 92, 94, 96

R

rabbi 78, 82
racial discrimination 27
rak'ah 95
Ramadan 88, 96
rasuls 87
reconciliation 62
Red Crescent 35
Reform Jews 12
Reformation 53
relative morality 50
religious leaders 2
religious order 51
repentance 48
requiem mass 64
Responsa 74
resurrection 45, 64, 70, 81
retribution 38
revelation 4
riba 93
Richard and Judy 43
risalah 87
Rite of Communion 60
rites of passage 52, 80
Roman Catholic Church
11, 14, 15, 18, 21, 53, 54
rosary 62
Rosh Hashanah 77, 83
ruh 13
rule of law 38
Ruth 29

S

Sabbath 47, 60, 82
sacrament 21, 55, 62
sacred writings 2
Sadaqah 35
salah 7, 86, 95
Salvation Army 53, 63
sanctity of life 14, 15
Sanhedrin 70
Satan 6, 7, 8
Saul 72
saviour 52, 65
Sawm 7, 86, 96
sa'y 96
scientific truth 2
search for meaning 3
Sefer Torah 78
Sephardic Jews 76
sermon 60, 64
Sermon on the Mount 49
Shabbat 82
shadchan 22
shahadah 7, 86, 95
shalom 40
shari'ah 92, 93
Shavuot 84
Shaytan 7, 9, 41
Shema 6, 73, 79, 81
Sheol 12, 81
Shi'ite 90, 94
shirk 86
shiva 81
Shoah 75
shroud 81
Shrove Tuesday 61
Simchat Torah 84
sin 38
Six-Day War 40
skip 63
skull cap 79
soap operas 43
Solomon 72
soul 1, 11, 12, 13
special revelation 4
spiritual truth 2
spirituality 1, 58
spontaneous worship 54, 60
squirrels 37
stained-glass window 58
stereotypes 27, 43
sterilisation 17
stewardship 36
storge 47
suffering 8, 9, 75
Sufism 91
suicide 15, 16
Sukkot 84
Sunday worship 60
Sunnah 88, 92
Sunni 90, 94
surah 88
symbolism 58
synagogue 31, 78, 82

T

tabernacle 60
Tabernacles 84
tallit 79
Talmud 74, 77
tawaf 96
Tawhid 7, 86
Tawrat 87
tefillin 79
Temple 72
Ten Commandments 47, 77, 78
Tenakh 74
terrorism 38, 39, 93
The Shadows 12
The Simpsons 42
There's something about Mary 54
Third World 34
tight-fisted 35
tobacco 41
tolerance 29, 30, 31, 32
Torah 73, 74, 76, 77, 78, 82
total immersion 63
transcendent 5, 6, 7
transept 56
transfiguration 61, 65
transubstantiation 54, 60
Trevor Huddleston 27, 28
trinity 5, 6, 45
truth 2
Twelve Tribes 72
tzedaka 35
tzitzit 79

U

Ur 72

V

vasectomy 17
veganism 37
vegetarianism 37
viaticum 62
vicar 55
virgin birth 45
voice of God 2

W

war 39, 40
watchmaker theory 3
watershed 43
wealth 34, 35
wedding 20, 22, 23, 57
Weeks 84
Welfare State 48
Western Wall 83
whirling dervish 91
Whitsun 61
will of Allah 13
wudu 86

Y

yahrzeit 81
yarmulka 79
Yawmuddin 13
Yhwh 73
Yom Kippur 77, 83

Z

zakah 7, 35, 86, 95
Zionism 73